DISCARD

MODERN GERMAN PAINTING

MODERN
GERMAN PAINTING

BY

HANS KONRAD ROETHEL

TRANSLATED FROM THE GERMAN
BY DESMOND AND LOUISE CLAYTON

REYNAL & COMPANY, NEW YORK

" *If one starts from the situation of modern natural sciences in order to grope towards the shaking foundations, it may not be an oversimplification to state that man on this earth, for the first time in history, is faced only by himself—he can no longer find any other partner or opponent.*"

Werner Heisenberg, Das Naturbild der heutigen Physik, Gestalt und Gedanke III (1954), p. 60.

TITLE PAGE: *Paul Klee* House by the Sea, 1920 Collection Richard Doetsch-Benziger, Basel

" Who wishes to be creative... must first destroy and smash accepted values."

However much the truth of these words of Friedrich Nietzsche may be doubted, they must nevertheless be accepted on historical grounds as having provided a beacon for the artistic revolution at the beginning of the 20th century. Possessed by an irrepressible *élan vital*, the modern artists felt themselves to be destroyers of the conventions surrounding them, and at the same time the augurs of new, unknown values. This holds true for the Fauves of France as well as for the Futurists of Italy. In Germany it was the members of the *Bruecke* and the artists the *Blaue Reiter* whose aims provided the foundation for the development of painting during the last fifty years. Despite all the differences in form, Beckmann, Kokoschka, and Corinth are also spiritually and intellectually related to Expressionism. The moderns did not only fight against traditional art forms. A new consciousness formed the basis of their attitude, and only in conjunction with the whole problem of existence could the artistic problem be solved, in heated debate and in urgent and frequently feverish creative impulses. Suddenly the work of art takes on a completely different importance relative to life. It is no longer commentary, imagery, a window into an imagined world; it seems to have escaped from the limitations of aestheticism and won a directness and autonomy formerly lacking. Robbed of its representative function in religion, expelled from its secure taken-for-granted position within the social hierarchy, it loses its illusionary character and becomes the direct, personal expression of its creator. It encounters a new society which is bound neither by sociology nor cult. Almost without pretext, without transition, and without hypocrisy, the new world of colour and form appears, and with what brightness, with what joyful directness the beauty of modern painting is revealed!

Manet's paintings, and those of the Impressionists, too, were still full of an

Paula Modersohn-Becker Self-Portrait with Camelia Branch, about 1907
Oil, 24″× 11″ Collection of Isermeyer, Hamburg

5

Erich Heckel Reclining Nude, 1909
Oil, 39″ × 49″ Bayerische Staatsgemälde Sammlungen, Munich

antipodal tension between the creative artist and the world; they still belong completely to the classical sphere of the " representative " arts. The question of " how " in the reproduction of the objectively perceived motif still takes first place before the aspiration towards a subjective avowal. Cézanne occupies a unique position.

The new idea, however, that distinguishes all modern art from that of the past 500 years is that the mere reproduction of existing objects and contents is replaced by the creation of pure forms, which, objective or not, as such, become expressions of beauty. The autonomy of the work of art, however, brings with it a change in the relationship between the spectator and the creation. Arbitrary aesthetic pleasure, through the medium of a refined sensitivity for formal values is replaced by a personal participation provoked by the work of art.

In the history of the *Bruecke*, Ernst Kirchner said, " With the belief in a development, in a new generation of creators as well as of spectators, we call upon youth to rally; to fight for elbowroom and for the right to live our own lives, away from the established older artists. All those belong to us who reproduce, direct and unadulterated, that which urges them to create." That is no aesthetic programme, no theoretical manifesto, not even an artistic credo in its narrower sense. It is the expression of a new consciousness of life.

They confronted the anemic intellectualism of a civilization self-complacently preening itself while threatened with suffocation in the materialism of a utilitarian belief in progress, with the belief in a new world, which, to them (to quote Nietzsche) still seemed " abundant in beauty, strangeness, doubt, horror, and divinity." Like Zarathustra they felt themselves " premature children of a yet unproved future." And despite the confusion, contradiction, and desperate need which made their first steps in the new direction so difficult, they were nevertheless convinced, in the passionate enthusiasm of their youth that through their work they would " create symbols which would take their place on the altars of the future intellectual religion." When Franz Marc, conscious of the general secession, wrote these words in the *Blaue Reiter*, he felt himself of one mind with the avant-gardist exponents of a new art of expression, to whose representatives, in his opinion, the Italian Futurists belonged just as much as Picasso and Chagall and the members of the *Bruecke*.

The Futurists, with their iconoclastic ideas, had displayed an almost hectic fanaticism. Exciting though their artistic language was, and despite the fact that their cultural criticism must be considered symptomatic of the then European situation, the extremism of their views was not so intimately related to the national temperament as were those of the Germans with Expressionism. The influence of their work was limited. In contrast to this the aspirations of the Fauves, the French " Savages," fused with the great artistic tradition of France, that happy country where even the most savage outsiders still preserve enough *raison* to allow their future inclusion in the spiritual Pantheon of their nation. Let us take Matisse, for example: " What I strive for, above all, is expression." That could just as easily have been said by the German Expressionists. But despite the solidarity of their intentions, despite the great similarity even in form, Matisse's art always retained that grain of *contenance* and that decorum that the German " savages " were fated to lose because they cherished more adventurous ambitions. In Germany, however, as has already been mentioned, Expressionism was at first a general term for all non-Impressionist, or more accurately, all anti-Impressionist art; it was retained as a slogan for a long time. Not altogether unjustifiably. For in spite of all the differences that had in the meantime become evident, the artists of the *Bruecke* and of the *Blaue Reiter* still had in common their cultural criticism, saturated with the spirit of Nietzsche, their faithful belief in a new world, their rejection of Impressionism, which they considered materialistic, and the vigour with which they strove towards their goal.

II

The nucleus of German Expressionism was the *Kuenstlergemeinschaft Bruecke*, which was formed in Dresden in the years 1903-1905. But in Germany, there was—as so often happens in that country, which through its multiformity and incoherence easily causes confusion—an artist who, though a complete individualist, must to a certain extent be considered the forerunner of this movement. It was Paula Modersohn-Becker. In the solitary village of Worpswede, surrounded by her artist friends who had withdrawn to this little moorland village not far from Bremen, she achieved a unique form of expression. The profound seriousness of the Worpswede people and the melancholy minor mode of their lives which pervade their paintings prepared the way to her achievement. But these painters were much too entwined in an objective reverence for nature to be concerned with the expressive power of form or colour as such. Paula Modersohn-Becker was to be freed from these bonds by her discovery of the French, late in her great and courageous life—in 1905-1906, only two years before her death. Cézanne and Gauguin, who had long been obscured for her by lesser masters, helped her in her last works to attain the form of a simple, great avowal, an independent womanly exposition of the plain and hard life which she read into the old people and children and reproduced with awe and compassion. However, in spite of the similarity of their intentions, there was certainly no effective influence on the aims of the Dresden group, be it by lack of personal contact or by too great a dissimilarity of their paths. The incubation period of the *Bruecke* appears to have been full of enigmas, confusion, and lack of clarity. Exactly when the community was formed or who its initiator was can not be accurately determined.

Ernst Ludwig Kirchner, Erich Heckel, and Karl Schmidt-Rottluff form the nucleus of this group of artists. Max Pechstein and Otto Mueller joined somewhat later. This is not the place to mention the names of the other active and passive members with the exception of Nolde, who, however, only belonged to the community as a guest for two years; they have only a marginal importance for German Expressionism. One is given the impression that in the midst of the overpowering events to which

Karl Schmidt-Rottluff Self-Portrait, 1910
Oil, 33″× 30″ Gallery Ferdinand Moeller, Cologne

Ernst Ludwig Kirchner Dancing School, 1914 Oil, 46″× 46″ Dr. Rüdiger Graf von der Goltz, Düsseldorf ▷

they were exposed, full of emotion and with a thirst for life, full of the ecstasy of common ideas, there was no room for reflection, for order, for reason. The events of the first few years, as can be seen from the available documents and from the later disputes and descriptions, are tinged with the kind of esotery, of collective witchcraft, which can easily develop in such a community founded on an emotional basis. The community savours of proletarian aristocracy, of romantic idealism and artistic anarchism.

ODI PROFANUM VULGUS—I hate the uninitiated masses—was the motto of their common life and work. When, with their characteristic mixture of passionate aggressiveness and provocative revolutionary spirit, they hurled the challenge of their revelations at that world of Prussian Victorianism where the absolute values were only allowed a carefully tamed existence in approved civilized costume, only

passionate hate and passionate love remained. The arrow shot by the German "savages" had scored a bull's-eye...

In Friedrichstadt, a working-class quarter in Dresden, not far from the railway marshalling yard, a vacant cobbler's workshop had been found and rented as a communal studio and home for the group. They made the furniture themselves; the stools were handcarved, the walls covered with painted and unpainted canvas. This concern for craftsmanship, for personal expression and artistic unity even in the everyday environment, was surely due to the influence of Fritz Schumacher, the distinguished architect and town planner, who at that time taught at the Dresden Academy of Art. He was professor of free-hand drawing, and later said about the early days of the *Bruecke* people, " In my horror at the messy drawing of those students, I could not pretend to understand the young ducklings who swam away from me, unexperienced mother hen that I was. But if I remained doubtful for the time being about the artistic value, I had on the other hand a definite feeling for the human value..."

Kirchner, Heckel, and Schmidt-Rottluff at first started to study architecture with Fritz Schumacher, but soon gave it up in order to devote themselves entirely to painting. Apart from Pechstein then, who had been working at the Dresden Academy from the beginning of the century, all the main representatives of the *Bruecke* were self-taught. In their blind rejection of everything academic they had probably not even noticed that hardly any of the German Impressionists would have been more suitable to further the development of their artistic ideas during the first few years than Gotthard Kuehl, who after a ten-year stay in Paris had been teaching in Dresden since 1895. But they would have turned their backs on Gotthard Kuehl just as they did on Fritz Schumacher. The new era was to be radical—had they not coined the phrase " Art depends on inspiration, not on technique." In the light of this attitude it is understandable that the principles of Expressionism can not be sought solely, or even primarily, in the fine arts. The vital renaissance of art was in direct correlation with the renaissance of life. A flood of reforms of all kinds had started suddenly since the beginning of the century. Their advocates tried to put a stop to the materialism and decadence of the *fin de siècle*—some using reason, intelligence, and a dash of common sense, others philistinism and irrational remedies. There were, to mention just a few, the *Goethebund* (1900), Karl Fischer's youth movement and the *Wandervogel*, the Art Teachers' Conference in Dresden (1901), the Darmstadt artists' colony (1901), Ferdinand Avenarius' *Duererbund* (1902), Johann Mueller's " Sanctuary " (1903), and last but not least, the *Werkbund* (1908)—they were all symptoms of the innumerable and varied efforts at all social levels to reform the whole system. Adventurous by-products like spiritualism and hypnotism joined up with new *Weltanschauungen* like the anthroposophy founded by Rudolf Steiner which introduced itself as the philosophy of the recognition of spiritual worlds. We can not concern ourselves here with the literary trends, with Dostoevski, Ibsen, Strindberg, Halbe, Wedekind, or with the early Gerhart Hauptmann whose works penetrated into hitherto unsearched depths of man's nature. The writings of Sigmund Freud had begun to appear after 1900. They form a fundamental part of the developing modern thinking and his philosophy has perhaps its most evident parallel in the libidinous paintings of the *Bruecke*. In music, Arnold Schoenberg's twelve-tone system provided a complete break with the harmony of the past. In 1910 Béla Bartók wrote *Allegro barbaro*.

In the fine arts, *Art Nouveau* was the promising beginning of a new form. Munich and Dresden were the main focal points. In 1906 Fritz Schumacher had organized the important Arts and Crafts Exhibition in Dresden. It was a triumph for *Art Nouveau*. But important though this movement was in that it broke away from the sham historical styles of the past, and creative as the new starting point must be considered, since man is used once more in his entirety as the basis of artistic ideals, so much less did it correspond to the ideals of the Expressionists. Its lifeblood was too thin after all; its realm was purely decorative ornamentation, and so it died like an anemic child, fell into the hands of commercialism and became degraded into a luxury article for the upper middle classes. Schumacher's rebel pupils, however, were not concerned with " domestic culture " or with tasteful cutlery. They considered that *Art Nouveau*, like most of the other movements to reform life and art, smacked somewhat of a kind of faith healing aimed at artificially extending the life of the moribund bourgeois aesthete.

The rebels were charged with different, more dangerous powers which demanded expression and shape: powers which built up into a mighty flood wave which even the rebels themselves did not fully understand. Ominous cracks began to appear in the apparently well-regulated world, streams of unconsciousness began to flow. The new truth showed up the threadbare quality of the old hybrid world. Suburbia, the prisoners, insanity, the troubles of childhood, disease as a natural part of human existence, were

Ernst Ludwig Kirchner Self-Portrait, circa 1918
Oil, 37″ × 33″ Staatliche Kunsthalle, Karlsruhe

recognized; weakness and fragility were admired. The potential beauty of ugliness was recognized. Not ugliness for its own sake, not as a distorted picture of humanity; it seemed to them that ugliness possessed a greater power of revelation, a purer core of truth, than traditional beauty. Just as a reflection of humanity can be seen even in abnormalities, just as even the gutter invokes our compassion at times, so can ugliness be loved for its inherent humanity. The old ideas of harmony disintegrated. Disorder disturbed the consciousness. Gloom, carnality, and the darker side of life forced themselves into the glare of daylight to establish a deeper reality.

The rebels no longer saw nature as a mere delight to the eyes or as the florescence of cosmic order; threatening clouds, the cruel sea, demonized trees and mountains or shrill skies became the features of their nature pictures. Unsuspected powers are found even in flowers. Hothouse plants develop into vampire-like growths, glowing with sensuality. Or they become, over and above their botanical qualities, with their radiant colours, the symbols of erotic glory. The world of visible things is shattered by the eruption of feeling, stripped of its pretty appearance; a naked world of animal impulses is given artistic expression.

On the one hand the grandeur of the North German Plain and the keen salty air of the North Sea, on the other hand the modern city with its stone web of streets, its urgency, its prostitutes, its steel bridges and canals, its music halls and its misery: city and sea, these were the most powerful stimulants for the Expressionists. These opposite extremes are felt to be one; man, as the creation of an unknown God is exposed to the onslaught of these new forces which he tries to assimilate. There was no room left for half, or apparent, truths. The pose of the Bohemians, whose libertinism was condoned by society, was despised. Life and art were to be one. They thought they should not allow themselves anything approaching poetic licence in either. The absolute was the criterion for everything. Their depressing pathos, their flagellant behaviour, their longing to revalue society, their inciting demonstrations, and their brutal attitude towards all aesthetic questions: all these characteristics sprang from the volcanic vitality and the revolutionary artistic drive of these new "savages."

The primitive force of these animal impulses now became an intrinsic part of artistic expression. Not in the sense that amorous themes were used. There has been no pornography, in fact, since Expressionism. Sensuality is virtually absorbed in the creative process, painting itself is charged with erotic potency. Nolde spoke of the burning impulse in his creations and demanded that the spectator should share his intoxication.

And yet—after all, it must be admitted—there was a pinch of proletarianism and a hint of the slums in their production. They did not always reach the stars on the wings of their passionate ambition, and the great idea was occasionally corruptively masked by the vision of a nudists' paradise. There is a puberal atmosphere about German Expressionism.

The beginning of modern German art is not altogether free of that heavy feeling of depression of whose victims Thomas Mann had his Tonio Kroeger say: "They become pathetic and sentimental; there is something clumsy, unironic, dull, and trivial about their work."

But we have already mentioned that they painted with a spontaneity of feeling that came straight from the heart—and the heart is not intelligent. But when it was able to exercise its power to the full, pictures were produced that can still move us today with their glowing vitality.

The Impressionists used their eyes as highly sensitive instruments to take in only the superficial quality of the perceptible world, and the artist reproduced the subjective impression of what he had seen. Colour was a substratum of nature, and later, by the Neo-Impressionists, it was even physically analyzed in order to aid artistic expression. The Expressionists, however, were not concerned with representing the appearance of the world, but with the dynamic forces to whose existence this appearance bore witness, or, to put it more accurately, with those forces which they thought they could sense behind the appearance. Their object was not the formal reproduction of perceptible data, but the artistic projection of an introspective image, the expression of a spiritual experience kindled by reality.

This produced a completely new relationship between subject and object. Impressionism demands an observant subject. Expressionism admits no a priori disposition of the person. August Macke said: "What we are, our I, must be re-created by us every moment." In other words, the Expressionists' ego only realizes itself in the work. "Rules do not exist outside the individual," wrote Matisse. The

◁ *Erich Heckel* Glassy Day, 1912-13   Oil, 48″×36″   Collection Markus Kruss, Berlin

creative I becomes autonomous. Things are to be lent a new meaning and importance. Without being bound to given conditions, whether imposed by nature or religion, these artists project their own being into the creation. This " self-projection " has its correlation in their impulsive productions. The dare-devilry, the *coûte que coûte*, in the creation of their pictures is conditioned by this egocentricity. At the same time, man is not a biological machine or civilized puppet, neither is he a product of a humanistic education, but in contrast to vaccilating atheists just as much as to conventional Christians, he feels himself to be a humble creation of an unknown God.

Of course they hated their elders. So they looked for their inspiration and forefathers far from everything civilized and academic. The untamed quality of the late Gothic wood carving, with its generous clarity of line, penetrating narrative power, and stylization bordering on vulgarity, which Kirchner had discovered for himself in Nuremberg, was regarded by them to be just as important a historical justification of their ideals as the dramatic art of Matthias Gruenewald or El Greco —both really discoveries of the Expressionists.

In their search for the primitive they discovered negro plastic art. It was not only the formal qualities that attracted and impressed the Expressionists, nor was it the bizarre and exotic as such; it was the strangeness and power of those sculptures and carvings that gave them their affinity to the Expressionist mentality. This affinity, however, has no aesthetic basis; it lies in the similarity of the creative act itself: neither the Negroes nor the Expressionists made an analytic study of the human figure the basis of their work. All that was denied (should we say fortunately?) to the Negro as a result of his evolutionary history—namely the rational Western education as it has developed from the Egyptian discovery of measurement to the theory of relativity—was rejected by the Expressionists. Their art was also born of an irrational, synthetic creative urge.

In addition to these idols of the past and of other continents, there were the great contemporary artists, Vincent van Gogh, Paul Gauguin, and Edvard Munch. The artists of the *Bruecke* were, according to Fritz Schumacher, quite beside themselves with excitement when they first saw some of van Gogh's pictures in 1906. Their ideals, vague at first, found realization here simply through the excitement, through what they felt to be " the directness and lack of dilution." Considering the spontaneity of the brush technique, what sublime subtlety in the use of colour, what crystal-clear proportions and what awareness of the quality and importance of light! As has been said, van Gogh was an Expressionist using Impressionist methods, but it was this very characteristic that provided such stimulation for the *Bruecke* artists and helped them to formulate their ideas. It was the dynamic animation, the definite form of van Gogh's pictures that appealed to them. The spectator was no longer presented with ephemeral manifestations of nature such as the Impressionists produced; a colourful, luminous titillation for the eyes was no longer enough: out of the vibrating green of the countryside rose the tree, an expressive creation, a form suggestive of its spiritual content.

Paintings by Gauguin were shown at the same exhibition, 1906. Here German artists found the simple life that they were after—that world of solemn dreams of innocence where mankind still lived in the purity of its primitive state, full of melancholy passion. What Gauguin had felt about the women of the South Sea Islands matched the ideas of the German " savages ": " It is Eve after the Fall, unashamed of her nakedness, still revelling in her animal beauty as on the first day." Gauguin was of prime importance in the artistic development of the *Bruecke* style. His palette, with its smoky reds with violet undertones and its lemon yellows, and above all his complete rejection of the charm of a well groomed surface, his stress on shape-relationship and the overcoming of all luminous effects—these were the elements which the *Bruecke* artists used to serve their own purposes. And they did not only follow in his artistic footsteps; his flight from civilization into the fairy tale world of Tahiti aroused the same longing in them: in 1913 Max Pechstein went to Palau and in 1914 Emil Nolde went to the South Seas. But whereas Gauguin sought virginity and peace there, the Expressionists allowed themselves to be engulfed in the intoxicating atmosphere of the South Seas.

Although only recently Heckel and Schmidt-Rottluff have expressly stated that they did not see any of Edvard Munch's pictures during the first years, it is utterly impossible to imagine the development of Expressionism in Germany without the Norwegian painter. Artists' statements have never more than a relative value.

◁ *Otto Mueller* Gypsies   Oil, 61″×40″   Collection of Herbert Kurz, Wolframs-Eschenbach

15

The first Munch exhibition had already taken place on the invitation of the Berlin Artists' Association in 1892. It created a scandal and led to the formation of the Berlin Secession. Strindberg had already written about him in the *Revue Blanche* in 1896, and, after a number of pamphlets and essays, the first monograph was published by Piper in Munich in 1905. The macabre character of Munch's pictures and his impulsive use of flaring colours must be considered an integral part of Expressionist painting. More important, however, was his wood carving technique, with its dismissal of detailed shading in favour of an impressive harmony of black and white areas which conformed to the natural shape of the wood. Thus van Gogh, Paul Gauguin, and Edvard Munch really had established the theme upon which the German Expressionists improvised their own style.

Because of the closeness of their communal lives it is difficult to estimate the part that individual artists played in the development of the *Bruecke* style. In the first few years there was friendly co-operation, an intensive exchange of ideas. Their poverty was such that lithographic stones had to be reground and turned over to a friend after only a few prints had been made (even these had to be used for fuel only too often). Despite the lack of clarity in the details, however, one thing is evident: the *Bruecke* style of the years 1905-1910 has very little to do with what is generally understood under Expressionism. The first pictures, and above all the drawings, lithographs, and etchings of the years 1905-1907 are the remnants of a late, plein-air Impressionism. They are full of delicate, almost dancing tones, held together by loose, flowing lines. These may well have been prompted by the lithographs of Bonnard or Vuillard which were to be seen in magazines like *Pan*. Cézanne's strict logic or Hodler's monumental figures, examples of constructive architectural composition, were much too opposed to the naive temperament of the *Bruecke* group to have influenced them. They were brought into contact—and this in itself was almost a miracle considering the mentality of the *Bruecke* people—with the European situation through the Fauves. In 1905 Kees van Dongen, the Dutchman, together with Matisse, Derain, and others, had taken part in the now famous Fauves Exhibition in the *Salon d'Automne* in Paris. He was a member of the *Bruecke* since 1906 and so might have been a direct link with Matisse. Kirchner's painting *Fraenzi-Seated* of 1907 appears to have been strongly influenced by Matisse's tones. Derain's *Trois personnages assis sur l'herbe* displays the same explosive power.

In the following year, it is true, both Kirchner and Schmidt-Rottluff still produced those wildly daubed landscapes which, with their patches of colour and atmospheric transparency, are in a direct line of development from Impressionism, though possessing considerably more temperament. But Heckel's *Reclining Girl* of 1909 shows the decisive change from spot to shape, from vague outline to grand contour. The *Bruecke* style, however, was not fully developed until 1910. The Exhibition of Rejects from the Berlin Secession was a milestone in the development. The " rhythm of their compact form," as Kirchner called it, became more urgent and passionate. The desire for expression, which, and this is a recurring characteristic in German art, sacrifices form to content, becomes evident in their use of shrilly dissonant and intense masses of pure colour and masterful contours. With wild brush strokes, with an almost aquarelle technique, all intermediate tones are ignored, all details are concentrated into great form complexes and all the components of the picture reduced to a few striking accents.

Ernst Ludwig Kirchner considered himself the leader of the group, and, even if this rightful claim was justifiably challenged during the first few years, he had the most passionate temperament, and that alone would be enough to win him a privileged position within the *Bruecke*. His *Seated Painter*, as the picture was originally called, is a self-portrait. He stares out of the picture as if hunted by invisible spirits, transfixed and transfixing, calling out and demanding answer. The egocentricity, the burning desire to communicate, the impulsiveness, the hand that appears to be guided by some magic power, but above all the eyes, unseeing, reflecting some inner light: these characteristics make the work a paradigm of Expressionist art. After the group had moved to Berlin, 1911, an extraordinary Gothic tendency emerged. This may well have been encouraged by a new preoccupation with the wood carvings of the late Middle Ages and by a leaning towards Cubist composition—Cubist composition, however, without its analytic dissection. Kirchner's brilliant street scenes, with their awkward pointed shapes, as well as the airy floating quality of his *Dancing School*, are characteristic of this stage of development. The painter took refuge from his war-ravaged country in Switzerland after a nervous breakdown in 1916; in the peace of the countryside his spirit recovered. The details of the pictures, no less passionate, now seem even more disciplined, more consciously arranged, and the whole takes on a festive orchestral colour. The theme is not a pastoral idyl; it is the ancient melancholy motif of an alpine shepherd race. In his last works, Kirchner forsakes the original ideas and aims of the *Bruecke* and tries to follow the *École de Paris*.

Max Pechstein Still Life, about 1913
Oil, 42″ × 28″ Kunsthalle, Mannheim

Karl Schmidt-Rottluff in his robust way is in complete contrast to the high-flying and restless Kirchner. He has a great flair for form and resembles Picasso in the sureness of his diction and in his naïve impulsiveness. His figures often seem about to burst out of their frames. A braced structure sometimes over-emphasized, but always full of tension, determines the geometry of his pictures. Dry, large and uncom-promising, stable, and intensely dynamic, the pictures leap out at us. Their virility is infectious. What a master of form he is, unrelenting and mercilessly determined! There is a barbaric *noblesse* in every one of his creations. And yet this rough hand can paint a blossoming sprig of chestnut so that one senses not only the primordial power of germination, but the soft zephyr-like charm of love.

Then there is Erich Heckel, milder and more delicate, more at home with the gentler contrasts of green and yellow than with the extremes of red and blue, more introvert than his two friends of the Dresden period. The pathos of the revolt is alleviated in his case by a streak of melancholic resignation. The older he gets, the more his palette turns to silver greys. He is more sensitive to light. He does not use colourful shadows, dancing sunlight, or an atmospheric tonality, but rather creates a colourful " light complex " as a whole. In *Glassy Day* of 1913, figure and landscape blend into a single "sonorous, magical space composition." The lake is not intended to be natural water, nor the sky, whose blue is painted with the same brush, a copy of the firmament. The glacial cloud-patterns dispense with all illusionary effect. The theme of the picture is not the radiance of a hot sunny day, or the cool blue of the lake; it is not a nude in a landscape, or morning or evening; it is jingling brittleness, prismatic fragility. It is the girlishness in the poetic harmony of landscape, clouds, figure, and blueness of lake and sky.

In 1910 Otto Mueller joined the group. He is the most lyric of the Expressionists and shares an almost brittle sensitivity with Heckel. His range is limited. He always paints slender sisterly girls, those long-legged, delicate-breasted creatures, who appear to spring from the very earth like the grass around them. Despite their intimate interrelationship and their closeness to nature, there is a feeling of loneliness about them. Grey-green pastel tones which deepen into dark blue on the contours of the graceful bodies, and bloodless, almost colourless lips, combine with the mat colours of nature so that everything visible seems to have withdrawn behind a veil of longing and scepticism. The painter's love for this promising world of puerile beauty is melancholically conscious of its limitations.

It seems as if Otto Mueller, out of a kind of over-sensitive conscientiousness, has fettered his own power of expression. His anti-bourgeois pathos, with the pride of being different, boasts of its identity with the ostracized. In his gypsy pictures the outcast becomes a vehicle of beauty. Despite the rags, despite the pipe in the mouth, despite the emaciation, the humanity of the Mother of Christ reaches its consum-mation in the Gypsy Madonna and is purer and truer than in the Nazarene, tawdry pictures of contem-porary religious art. His admiration of ancient Egyptian works is reflected in his tendency to archaistic severity. His dry colours, his glimmering reds, and the emphasized outlines of his figures went a long way, with Schmidt-Rottluff's strength and Kirchner's impulsiveness, to crystallize the *Bruecke* style after 1910. Max Pechstein played a less important part in the communal life of the *Bruecke* and did little to help towards the development of the *Bruecke* style; yet he worked along the same lines in the early years of the group.

The move to Berlin starts the gradual end of the unity within the group. The *Chronicle of the Bruecke*, written in 1913, marks the obvious close. But though the human contact becomes less intimate, the individual members—through the mutual recognition of their work, and spurred by the shattering ex-periences of the First World War—develop a very pregnant form of artistic expression, which, in its " Expressionism " forms an integral part of modern German art.

Apart from the *Bruecke*, to which he only belonged for two years as a guest, Emil Nolde is the most notable phenomenon of German Expressionism. Except for the great wood carvers of the late Middle Ages like Bernt Notke and Claus Berg, no one had succeeded in so revealing the stubborn, ponderous and inarticulate soul of the picture-less North. All the latent power of his race is released in this brood-ing, tenacious artist from Northern Germany. The way from his peasant environment to the regions of art led through the cramping professions of arts and crafts teacher and pattern designer. Early cari-catures of giant mountains are the first signs of escape from the stolid world of copy work, and introduce a scurrilous and grotesque element into the creative field which is later continued in the form of masks, idols, and distorted faces. About 1908 he finally finds himself, discovers colour. The mentality of the *Bruecke* may have been his inspiration—not its form as such, but the emotional attitude and the ideals that gave it birth. The seething and foaming colours are made to yield the utmost passion. They pour over the canvas like lava, but a closer look reveals the significant discipline and shows how the form is

Emil Nolde Adoration
Oil, 41" × 55" Collection of Ernst Henke, Essen-Bredeney

born of itself. What an accumulation of conventions had to be cleared away, before the peculiar simplicity, the originality and magic of this domineering peasant could come into their own! The landscape is not revealed as something measurable, as something optically tangible; instead, its over-present primordial quality is charged with an exciting actuality through the medium of this fiery spirit. Flowers are transformed into colourful, splendid symbols, or appear like the carnal apparitions of a sensuous dream. And in the same way that nature in this sense is, dematerialized, so man is also stripped of all the by-products of civilization, and religious feelings are deprived of their sectarian façades.

Yet, the energies trammeled by tradition or convention have only a liberating effect on the painter; they evoke a spiritual state of mind. The religious picture is not constrained by dogma. Piety is looked upon as a basic human feeling, as a natural disposition of the soul. Thus Nolde's painting of the Last Supper or of the Adoration of the Kings will be neither a pictorial lesson in liturgy, nor, of course, a realistic representation of a " historical " situation. Instead it shows the human element, the psychological content; the spiritual aura which elicits sympathy is created with a piety borne out of the immanent faith of thousands of years: " Colours with a life of their own, laughing and crying, happy and dreamy, burning and holy, like love songs and eroticism, like melodies and magnificent chorales!——Colours that vibrate like silver and bronze bells, heralding happiness, passion, and love, spirit, blood and death " (Nolde).

Christian Rohlfs, similar to Nolde in background and character, may also be linked with him artistically. Certainly he has not the power of the latter, but his town scapes, his religious scenes, his dance compositions, and above all the flower pictures which he continued to paint in his old age, show a definite similarity of intent. Rohlfs is less aggressive in form and content. He is more delicate and groping and therefore also less definite in his diction. His resplendent colours seem to be mildly broken by the atmosphere or removed to the unreality of a dream. They recall the exordium in plein-airism, never quite relinquished. The expressive picture of *St. Patroclus in Soest* clearly illustrates this intermediate phase.

III

The Expressionism of the *Bruecke* artists and their friends was intellectually vernaculer to North German Protestantism. The mode of expression used by the members of the *Blaue Reiter*, saturated in the spirit of Nietzsche, was based on the same principles, even though their headquarters was in Munich. But

Emil Nolde Flowers and Clouds, 1938
Oil, 29″× 35″ Collection of Bernhard Sprengel, Hanover

Christian Rohlfs St. Patroclus in Soest ▷
Oil, 24″× 40″ Private Collection

Ernst Ludwig Kirchner Alpine Hut, 1917
Oil, 48" × 60" Staatliche Kunsthalle, Karlsruhe

however closely related their exordium might have been, wavering between despair and hope, the artistic results were entirely different. The two groups were united in their renunciation of the " easy usufruct of a romantic retrospection," in their rejection of the " vainglorious progressiveness of positivism," and not last in their resistance against the " rationalistic arrogance and frivolity," and the " mendaciousness of European morale." Their hate was directed especially against the " emptiness of the art routine, which isolates the artist just as much as it does the work of art," and, in the field of art itself, against Impressionism, which they felt to be a form of materialism. In this they were not altogether unjustified. But whereas the *Bruecke* members eruptively produced their passionate work from the depths of primitive emotion, the *Blaue Reiter* artists gained, through the speculative efforts of Kandinsky and the very nearly religious ethos of Franz Marc, a certain spiritual quality foreign to the other group. The *Bruecke* followers did not talk, they painted. Their works are like an outcry. The members of the *Blaue Reiter*, however, started from the intellect, they analyzed, philosophized. They were just as much interested in religious questions as in the developments in modern music, in the theatre, and in literature. Their curiosity in the startling discoveries of modern natural science, which, of course, they felt rather than considered, convinced them a priori that they were pioneering truth-seekers. What they heard about

22

those sciences, actually so remote from them, certainly was not the basis of their work as has been claimed, or even the reason of their artistic conception. But as the pioneers of a new world, as they felt themselves to be, they instinctively sensed something of the significance of the scientific revolution. They welcomed these discoveries as confirmation of the fact that the old world which they sought to overthrow was also "scientifically" unsound. In fact there is no causal dependence that connects the non-representational painting produced in their circle with microphysics, but there exists a structural relationship between theories on the objectivity of reality. Thus the *Blaue Reiter* artists were conscious of being on the brink of a dangerous future and they were courageously prepared to carry their share of responsibility. That imparted the glory of young heroes to them: "Many who are not filled with an inner passion will freeze and withdraw to the ruins of their memories" (Franz Marc).

Apart from their artistic aims, and apart from the ethos, the spiritual quality, and their characteristic confidence, the *Blaue Reiter* artists differed from the *Bruecke* group above all in that they did not pursue

Karl Schmidt-Rottluff Mediterranean Harbor, 1928
Oil, 39″× 44″   Collection of Hanna Bekker vom Rath, Hofheim

a communal existence. Munich, that Janus-faced town, where ruralism and cosmopolitanism peacefully mingle, was the meeting ground of those artists, who, as varied as they were by background and education, first proclaimed their unity in the "New Artists' Association" and later in the activities of the *Blaue Reiter*. During the last decade of the 19th century new forces were already stirring with the result that Munich's fame as a cradle of the arts no longer rested on the legendary era of Ludwig I or as a mere arena for the platitudes of old masters. The realm of the powerful leading artist, Franz von Lenbach, was considerably shaken by the forming of the Secession in 1893 (the same year in which Thomas Mann moved to Munich). Franz von Stuck, Fritz von Uhde and Gotthard Kuehl were among the leaders of the new group. Arnold Boecklin, Louis Corinth, Max Liebermann, Max Slevogt, Wilhelm Truebner and Adolf Hoelzel also exhibited in the Secession's first show in Prinzregentenstrasse. At the same time Hermann Obrist displayed his embroideries, dainty floral ornaments which just as obviously rejected Renaissance eclecticism as they exhibited a new feeling for form. *Art Nouveau* put forth its first shoots. In 1894 Otto Eckmann had his paintings, which he ironically called his "artistic legacy," publicly auctioned. Easel painting in the old style was to be buried once and for all. The magazine *Pan* (1895-1900), especially the aptly named *Jugend* (Youth) as well as *Simplicissimus* (both have appeared in Munich since 1896). In 1898 August Endell designed his phantastic, ludicrous façade ornament for the Elvira Photographic Studio, and in 1901, Richard Riemerschmid built the Munich *Schauspielhaus*, one of the most successful theatre buildings in the world.

The fermenting atmosphere of Munich during the nineties attracted art-smitten yourths from Chicago to Moscow to the banks of the Isar. In 1896 Alexej von Jawlensky came with Marianne von Werefkin; Kandinsky followed in 1897; they studied with Anton Azbe. In 1898 Kubin and Klee arrived. Then Bechtejeff and the Burljuk brothers joined the Russian colony—to mention the names of only the most important artists that came from afar to join the intimate circle of the *Blaue Reiter*. In 1909 Kandinsky, with his Russian friends and Gabriele Muenter, Adolf Erbsloeh, Alexander Kanoldt, and others, formed the "New Artists' Association." Their first exhibition took place that winter. A rather confusedly for-

Franz Marc The Great Blue Horses, 1911
Oil, 40″ × 63″ Walker Art Center, Minneapolis, Minnesota, U.S.A.

Franz Marc Two Horses, about 1912-1913 Tempera, 15″× 13″ Rhode Island School of Design, Providence, R. I., U. S. A.

Franz Marc Tirol, 1913-14
Oil, 53″× 57″ Bavarian State Collection, Munich

mulated pamphlet issued at the foundation of the group was reprinted in the foreword to the catalogue. The group believed that the artist, apart from the impressions he receives from the objective world, should continually be gathering inner experience, and this total experience, freed of all irrelevance, should be formed into a new artistic synthesis. That was an old, romantic tune and a very tame slogan for the painting of the future. Seen in relation to the artistic situation of that time and to later events, it meant the rejection of the naturalistic plein-air painting, that form of German Impressionism which was cultivated by the Secession. At the second exhibition, held in the following year, Braque, Kees van Dongen, Picasso, Rouault, and Vlaminck appear as guests. Henri V. G. Le Fauconnier and Pierre Paul Girieud had become members. The international flavour was nothing new; it was in keeping with an old tradition of the *Glaspalast*, the famous exhibition hall in Munich. This exhibition provided the

26

first international general survey of the new movement. Burljuk in his foreword proclaimed the " spiritual relationship " with Cézanne, Gauguin, van Gogh, Matisse, and Picasso. The " archaic," and the " wonderful fairy-tale world of Scythian plastic art " were evoked; civilized refinement was to be confronted with the primitive and naive, with monumental grandeur. It was felt that these qualities in their pure form were to be found in the works of the primitive, and in folk art, rather than in the works of the leading masters. They attacked the adventitious character of the motifs used by the latter and their unnecessary thoroughness in the execution of details. They missed above all what they called the " spiritual experience," what Kandinsky was later to call " the spiritual in art." In the foreword to the catalogue of this exhibition, Kandinsky defined more clearly than in any other of his writings content and form of his artistic aims—though characteristically with a question mark: " The expression of secrets through secrecy—is that not the content? " This sentence should presage future events.

The preparations for the 1911 exhibition led to a split in the New Artists' Association. A few members demanded that their works should not be submitted to the jury. As this request was not met with, Kandinsky, Muenter, Kubin, and Franz Marc, the youngest member, withdrew from the group. This step was not the result of hurt ambitious pride, as artists' quarrels so often are. It was both artistically sensible and necessary. At the tea table in Maria Marc's house in Sindelsdorf, the little storm troop gave itself its name, full of yearning and stormy courage: *Der Blaue Reiter* (The Blue Rider). In fact this name meant only the editorial staff (Kandinsky and Marc) of an art almanac which, as such, published only that one volume dedicated to Hugo von Tschudi, 1912, and organized two exhibitions in Munich. They were afterwards taken over by Herwarth Walden as the opening exhibition for *Der Sturm* in Berlin, and later toured Germany.

The first exhibition organized by the *Blaue Reiter* took place in the Arco-Palais in Munich simultaneously with one organized by the New Artists' Association in the Thannhauser Gallery there. It consisted of 43 pictures and lasted only three weeks. Apart from Kandinsky, Marc, and Muenter, works by Burljuk, Macke, Campendonck, and Jean Niestlé were exhibited. Jawlensky and Werefkin, although artistically and personally closely connected with the *Blaue Reiter*, did not participate. Among the foreigners represented, Henri Rousseau, who had died the previous year, and the contemporary cobelligerent Delaunay, took first place. Arnold Schoenberg, the musician, was also represented by three works. The second exhibition, arranged a few months later (March-April 1912) consisted only of graphic art. All the *Bruecke* members were included as well as Klee, Arp, Braque, Derain, Malewitsch, Morgner, Nolde, and Picasso. This exhibition was anything but stylistically consistent; yet this avant-garde, which was everywhere to triumph over nationalism thus had declared its solidarity.

But what had happened in the art world?

The group of Russian artists had brought with them from their remote homeland (which later was to influence Rilke and Barlach so deeply) a strange spiritual ethos. They combined a revolutionary pathos with an introversion of emotions. In 1904 Kandinsky's meeting with the symbolism of the West led to a kind of sophisticatedly stylized fairy-tale illustrations; thus, for example in *Poésies sans Paroles*, a popular balladic element is mixed with the artful curvatures of an Aubrey Beardsley. In the same period a consolidation of his late-Impressionistic technique took place, in that his patches of colour which up till then had been stippled were now formally controlled in the style of Signac and appeared slightly sharpened in tone. The motifs, which are mainly landscapes, lack emotional content—it seems as if the curriculum of European painting since Cézanne had to be caught up on. In the Murnau period the creative character of his works becomes autonomous. A tree trunk, for example, may still resemble its natural appearance, but being painted yellow it no longer has any representational value. The colour scale has become an independent element of the picture's organism. In 1908 Kandinsky and Gabriele Muenter acquired a house in Murnau; at the same time Jawlensky moved there with Marianna von Werefkin. They had gained an insight into the fluxible situation of painting everywhere by their long journeys throughout Europe and extended stays in Paris. But in Murnau, where they would look at the great range of the mountains, and lived so close to the beloved waters of Lake Staffel, here in the pleasant foothills of the Bavarian Alps, everything learnable and sought-after seemed to be forgotten. Somewhere in their artistic consciousness memories of Russian folk art encountered Bavarian backside glass paintings which they could still see painted in the traditional style before their eyes in Murnau. The colourful dreams of youth unexpectedly came across an ancient practice long perfected. It is true that Matisse influenced them indirectly through his emancipation of colour. But these darksome landscapes that were now painted with such verve by Kandinsky, Muenter and Jawlensky are in their naïveté,

August Macke Walk on the Bridge, 1913
Oil, 20″× 22″ Collection of Bernhard Koehler, Berlin

their brilliant freshness, their simplicity and depth, certainly original creations. They launched the march for the *Blaue Reiter*. What Kandinsky worked out step by step with much reflection seems to have been achieved with all the force of her naive absoluteness almost playfully by Gabriele Muenter in one happy moment. Jawlensky's approach had much in common with Muenter's. Even he, the former captain of a Russian grenadier regiment, created more freely, was less controlled and complicated than the methodical Kandinsky. But it was he who followed in Muenter's footsteps rather than the reverse. Areas of stronger, deeper colour outlined in black represent mountains, fields, trees, and houses. The brush technique is fast and relaxed, often refreshingly carefree; the pictures seem improvised, like inspirations of the moment. The character of these landscapes is determined not by the compact instrumentation of the usual palette, not by endless nuances of light and shade, the variety of foliage, grass, and branches, but by the harmony of penetrating tones not so dependent on sculptural factors, and by clearer form accents. Certainly

August Macke   Sailboats, 1910   Oil, 28″×20″   Collection of Mr. and Mrs. Sigmund Heumann, New York

Wassily Kandinsky Rider-Improvisation 12, 1910
Oil, 38"× 41" Bavarian State Collection, Munich

one should not be too rash in declaring that the "essence" of the landscape has been given shape by these things just because they have succeeded in reducing the multiplicity of the visible world to a few optical formulae. They are pictures that daringly reject the naturalistic pictorial representation of real things; their importance lies in their expression of a simple and great feeling that is reflected in nature. This applies above all to Muenter and Jawlensky. Muenter had already found her artistic province, and it was to remain practically unchanged. Jawlensky developed strangely through his contact with the *Bauhaus*, which is reflected in his many variations on two themes—the landscape and the human face. But on closer examination how much more complicated are Kandinsky's pictures of this early Murnau period! Although his paintings are less emotional than Muenter's and Jawlensky's works, less warm and radiant, his colour composition is more accomplished and daring. The even arrangement of the picture's elements turns into a varied tension. Taut patches of red, in contrast to the dispersed cold green of a tree shape, form here explosive centers of energy. The brush stroke, sometimes stippled, sometimes in controlled parallel lines, is subordinated in length, direction, strength, and liveliness to the organization of the painting. That was inherited straight from Cézanne. One can sense in these pictures the future still fettered, but impatiently striving to free itself.

In addition to the landscapes, Kandinsky also produced *Improvisations*, like strange colourful tapestries that tell of riders, cupolas, and women, of swords and goblets. They are almost songs without words which express old feelings in new tunes, the content never quite comprehensible, never unequivocally descriptive, purplish iridescent like an old legend. Some pictures from this period (like *Ladies in Hoop Skirts*, 1909), due to their subjects, have a certain sentimental paleness about them, a smack of sophisticated, fashionable *Art Nouveau*. One should not lose sight of his earlier subjects when judging the possible content of his later works. Despite their abstract quality they still retain a good portion of rash boyishness. However that may be, the formal development seen in its infancy in the *Improvisations* is of great importance for the conquest of a new world of forms.

To define his intuitively felt aims as simply as possible: "tenderness" was no longer to be restricted to the genre-like representation of an embrace, nor "animation" to the concrete portrayal of a dance, but the whole endless realm of spiritual half tones and intermediate tones, from the ominous and inarticulate to the robust tutti furiosi, was to be given artistic shape through the purely abstract vibration of colour and form. This,

Franz Marc   Fighting Forms, 1914
Oil, 38" × 52"   Bavarian State Collection, Munich

Gabriele Muenter At Sunset, 1909
Oil, 18½″× 26½″ Collection of the Artist

however, was no mere logical possibility or theoretical idea such as had been cherished by romantics like Philipp Otto Runge and Novalis; it was a perfectly legitimate thought artistically. Its realization needed the utterly faithful affection with which Kandinsky devoted himself to what had been unimaginable before. Kandisky had told Gabriele Muenter as early as 1905, long before he had grasped his artistic aims, that even as a student he had already found the subject matter of his paintings more of a disturbance than a help (Eichner). The basic conditions necessary for abstract painting had already been created by the colour experiments and the work on composition problems of the Neo-Impressionists. Looking back, already van Gogh and Seurat had started to come to grips with these problems that were later to be solved by Kandinsky as a morphological consequence. There had been many concrete attempts in the direction of abstract painting; in Munich, Hoelzel had tested artistic mediums for their independent values, though more by way of experiment. Endell had theorized about them. The Munich Jugendstil was Kandinsky's most important and at the same time most dangerous forerunner. One only needs to recall the independent power of line as had been formulated by van de Velde. " A line is a force, borrowing its force from the energy of its drawer." This provided a fruitful beginning. Nobody was more aware than Kandinsky of the danger of petrifaction at the ornamental stage, and his development quite distinctly shows that he avoided this short circuit inherent in abstract art. Kandinsky himself mentioned the preliminary stages through which he passed: having seen one of Monet's *Haystacks* at the Impressionists'

Gabriele Muenter Kandinsky at the Tea-Table, about 1910-11 Oil, 70″×48½″ Collection of the Artist ▷

32

Paul Klee Senecio, 1922
Oil, 18" × 16" Museum of Art, Basel

◁ *Wassily Kandinsky* Improvisation, 1910 Oil, 27 1/4" × 18 7/8" Yale University Art Galleries, New Haven

Exhibition in Moscow, he unconsciously came to the conclusion that " the object was no longer an inevitable element of a picture." Wagner's *Lohengrin* made a lasting synaesthetic impression on him. " I saw all my colours; they stood before my eyes. Wild, almost crazy lines drew themselves before me... I realized that art in general is much more powerful than I had thought, and that painting could develop the same kind of powers that music possessed." And finally, as he said in his *Reminiscences* (1913), it was the news of the " splitting of the atom " that made him believe that science was destroyed. " Everything became insecure, shaky and soft."

In 1910, in Munich, at 36 Ainmillerstrasse, the first completely abstract aquarelle was created. What distinguishes this work, and the large " Improvisations " and " Compositions " produced before the First World War, from all earlier works of a similar kind is the convincing pictorial effect. In those years, Kandinsky was realizing his ideas with passionate verve, stimulated by the thought that he was conquering a new world. All his works of that period are the " abstract expressions " of wild animation, explosive in the seething upsurge of the forms, in the dynamic tension of the colours. They closely resemble the works of the *Bruecke* artists in their vitality. One can follow step by step the way in which the subject is effaced in these pictures. Certain abbreviated signs appear. The frequently repeated three parallel black lines are an example. They are a rudimentary form of the troika (in bird's-eye view). Certainly, this configuration does not " mean " a troika; it paraphrases in associative form a suppressed motif which originates from this object. There are a number of such fragments remembered, which have coagulated into hieroglyphic form: riders, water, saints, and the cupolas of Moscow. Although these signs as such are unknown to the uninitiated spectator, he senses, apart from the overwhelming events which present themselves directly as pure form, the import of the message. It is true that the picture, as far as the standard classification of the art work goes, is meaningless, without content. But that does not imply that the abstract work of art as a creation has not its own special significance. Kandindsky's early non-objective pictures possess such a high degree of artistic conviction because the vital experience is still present, no matter how cryptically formulated. It is sensible but not tangible. The gap between the content and the form (*Gestalt*) was to become a cesspool for uncontrolled interpretations. For this intangibility was as attractive as the forbidden fruit. And as the usual instruments of interpretation are no longer sufficient, the spectator becomes a poetaster and daringly postulates that the magic, the mystic, even the cosmic, have become the content of the pictures. That is not true. As has already been hinted at, the problem is the representation of definite spiritual tension-relationships which by their very nature can not be portrayed with definiteness but which can nevertheless be completed by the spectator through a kind of sensitive optical communion.

Kandinsky's early abstract paintings are the climax of his work. He was 48 years old at the outbreak of the World War. After abstract art has been created by the effacement of the subject matter, he approaches the resulting questions almost from the opposite point of view. He tries to create a grammar of painting through his work. In his research on the basic principles of colour and form he was to be supported by the members of the *Bauhaus*.

In Munich Franz Marc was his most understanding friend, who by good advice and creative assistance, but above all by the same faithful seriousness, helped to bring about the great change in modern German painting.

A native of Munich, he wanted to study like his elder brother philosophy, then theology. After having completed his military service, however, he changed his mind and became a painter like his father. Studying with Hackl and Diez in Munich brought him no satisfaction. An extremely emotional sensitivity and a fear of life heightened by insecurity and disappointment aggravated his restlessness and scepticism. This psychological condition provided the right basis for the study of Nietzsche, whose influence can be discerned in all of Marc's work, including his writings. His artistry was not founded on craftsmanship although the vivacious sketches of his youth offer such promising talent. He shows early signs of looking beyond mere picture-making. A notable success with an exhibition of naturalistic animal pictures does not prevent him from increasingly trying to get away from the " arbitrariness of colour." Behind this turning away from " desultory fumbling with light " (as he says in another place) was a demand for a criterion for art which should be of greater importance than the insignificant emotional content of the usual genre-painting and of greater importance than the " realities " of plein-airism: " Consider my friends, what pictures are; materialization in a different place." (" *Erkennt, meine Freunde, was Bilder sind: das Auftauchen an einem anderen Ort.*") As far as the pictorial effect is concerned, however, overcoming the " arbitrariness of colour " means the search for a form of expression in which the colour

Gabriele Muenter Man in an Easy Chair (Paul Klee), 1913
Oil, 37" × 49" Bavarian State Collection, Munich

through its latent magic power should appear as definite and unambiguous as possible. It may not be superfluous to mention that these are not objective laws for which artistic realization was sought, but subjective truths, the value of which was limited by space and time. Certainly they were truths, the importance of which may be compared to Goethe's theory of colour.

In 1910 Franz Marc discovered the New Artists' Association. Here were the people of his own mind whom he needed and had been looking for. He became a member. And when Kandinsky left the group, Marc, as has already been said, was among the few that followed him. The almanac had already been planned before this happened; it was to be " the organ of all the new and genuine ideas of our days." Then followed the *Blaue Reiter* Exhibition. In 1911 *The Great Blue Horses* were painted.

Marc loved animals. He had a good friend in his dog " Schlick "; he kept deer in his garden. " The impious people around me (above all the men)," he wrote from the front, " do not arouse my real feelings, while the animal's innocent attitude towards life evokes all that is good in me."

With Franciscan devotion he turned to the animal world. There he recognized the pure creation that fulfilled its destiny in sacrifice. Thus he did not see his animals with the eyes of a stalker; he rather stripped them of the adventitiousness of their natural existence in his paintings and elevated them to the sphere of sacred legends. His pictures are like the celebration of a message full of hope. The solemnity of the colours, the pure concord between the animals' bodies and the surrounding landscapes, and the

Alexej von Jawlensky The Red Scarf
Oil, 21″× 19″ Private Collection

simple greatness of the lyric atmosphere, create a kind of paradisiac fairy world, in which the animal, transfigured by an unresisting participation in the universe, becomes the expression of a religious feeling. Franz Marc painted animals neither as " existences," nor as " symbols." It is the aura of innocence emanating from the animal, the purity and goodness, which is given expression in his pictures. Blue, red, and

Alexej von Jawlensky Mountains (around Murnau), 1912
Oil, 21″ × 19″ Collection of Hanna Bekker vom Rath, Hofheim

yellow horses, red deer—in their intrinsic, joyful colourfulness which nevertheless does not exclude the possibility of ominousness, they all become artistic revelations of his mystic feeling of oneness with the universe.

Stimulated by his interest in the young European avant-garde, and driven by an inner necessity to bring his painting into line with what he understood under modern natural science, Franz Marc underwent a stormy development in the few years that were still granted him. " I could not reconcile modern science with my kind of art. It had to be done, however, and not *au détriment des sciences*, but with absolute respect for the European exact sciences. Science is the basis of our European civilization: if we really wish to have an art of our own it can not live against the findings of science."

Wassily Kandinsky   Street in Murnau, 1912   Oil, 27″× 49″   Private Collection, New York, N.Y.

Paul Klee   The Window, 1919   Water Colour, 10″× 25″   The Silbermann Gallery, New York, N.Y.

Wassily Kandinsky Composition, 1914
Oil, 40″× 31″ The Solomon R. Guggenheim Museum, New York, N.Y.

Paul Klee Composition, 1914
Tempera, 10″× 11″ Museum of Art, Basel

Wassili Kandinsky Composition in Red, 1924 28″× 17″ Collection of M. Sacher, Basel ▷

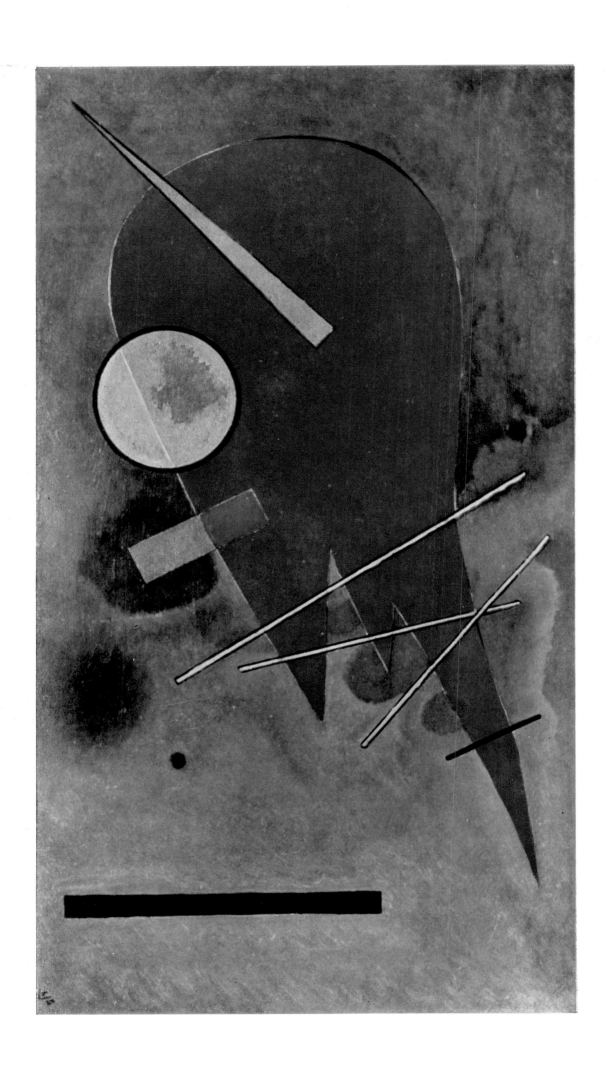

Paul Klee Mask, 1940
Pastel and Tempera, 10″× 11″ Klee Foundation, Bern

The painting *Tiger* (1912), one of his most daring and powerful creations, exhibits Cubist elements. The *Animal Fates* (1913) includes Futurist forms and thoughts. In the former the animal body is enclosed in a system of crystalline refraction. The latter is shot with angular pencils; plastic compactness is sacrificed in favor of two-dimensional dynamism, colourful beams of light stream across the picture with torrential force. The *Tower of Blue Horses* (1913, formerly National Gallery, Berlin, now disappeared) represents probably the acme of his work, and not merely in the sense of its "transfiguration" of the animal, but also—and principally—through the Gothic glorification of form as such. The simultaneity of Delaunay is modified, and the rhythmically intensifying colour concord of blue is brought to a solemn orchestral effect. "*Je cherche à me mettre dans un état de grand amour*" (I try to get myself into a state of great love), he wrote to his French friend in March 1913. The *Tower of the Blue Horses* is as European as it is German.

46

Though Franz Marc and Kandinsky agreed in their intellectual conception of Abstract painting, the paths by which they realized their aims were not the same, and the results also were as different as had to be expected from such diverse temperaments and characters. Line played scarcely any part in Marc's work and there is no hieroglyphic reduction of the objective motif. Marc thinks in terms of areas of colour which are full of crystalline refraction and overlap here and there—in accordance with the superimposed planes. Trees, houses, and cattle, resolutely enclosed within the colour structure, disappear into or appear like significant signals out of the kaleidoscopic sea of colour.

In 1914 Marc painted the series of " gay " and " playful ". "battling " and " broken forms." They are pure abstract pictures. In the *Battling Forms* the picture is based on the colour contrast between red and blue. There is a faint echo of the lineal lyricism of *Art Nouveau*. But the roaring colours are like the clashing of arms. The great colour monsters collide thunderingly. On the flanks the opponent is kept at bay by weaving curves. Flashing lunges, sharp and cutting, seem to illuminate the turmoil of forms... " But as it crashed together behind him, gardens appear again, and the sixteen curved sabres that spring upon him, flashing, are a feast. A laughing fountain..."

In 1914 Marc went to the front with the German army. In 1916 he fell at Verdun. During one of his leaves he worked his picture *Tyrol* over which he had painted in 1913, and added the Madonna. This picture, more so than the abstracts, even more than the pages of his frontline sketchbook with its *Magical Moment*, and the *Arsenal for Creation*, represents probably his artistic testament: the world of his beloved mountain landscape, transfigured by the vision of divinity.

Whereas the painting of Franz Marc and Kandinsky sprang from their volition and compulsion, with August Macke was above all a question of ability. He was more naive and perhaps more gifted. " Of all of us, he gave colour its clearest and purest tone, as clear and pure as his whole being was." That was written by Franc Marc of his friend who had been killed in France in 1914 at the age of 27. No matter how unnatural Kandinsky's theoretical speculations appeared to his naive artistic nature, and however sceptical his criticism was later of Kandinsky's artistic production, Macke nevertheless found himself at first very much in agreement with the *Blaue Reiter*. In 1910 he saw some of Marc's works at Brackl's in Munich, and consequently visited him. A spontaneous, warm-hearted friendship should develop out of that meeting. Macke had not yet found himself; his study in Duesseldorf and a few months with Lovis Corinth had borne no fruit. Trips to Paris together with Bernhard Koehler, the great collector and art patron, had widened his horizon and opened his eyes, but he was not yet able to integrate all he had seen. In 1909 he went to Tegernsee for a year with his young family. The exhibition of the New Artists' Association—especially the pictures of Muenter and Jawlensky—helped to indicate the way for him as it did for Marc. But he held himself aloof from the others: " For greatness I lack the self-evident." After Kandinsky and his friends had left the group Macke worked intensively with the others on editing the almanac. But only an oil—*Storm*—painted in Marc's attic studio at Sindelsdorf during the preparations for the almanac, gives artistic expression to the closeness of the united intellectual efforts.

After his first groping steps, which were just as instinctively sure as critical, the decisive experience of his life was Macke's meeting with Delaunay. In October 1912 he went with Marc to see him in Paris. It was like a revelation. For the sensuous Rhinelander Braque's or Picasso's analytic Cubism was just as alien as Kandinsky's abstractions. The Futurists, with their attempt to mirror a chronological sequence in their pictures, certainly exercised their influence on him. Yet in Delaunay, he found that warmly glowing, resplendent colour-mosaic which was to become the fulfillment of his own efforts. Although he was most convinced by Delaunay's principle of *fenêtres* (windows), because it liberated the " plastic energies of colour " one can not call him a disciple of " Orphism." How different is Macke's world! Quiet ponds; parks; slender women in long, narrow clothes; silent, congenial couples who, unworldly and full of dignity (like swans) walk together. And then the delicate figures of girl-like women in front of millinery shops, who, though interested in the frills of fashion, nevertheless indulge themselves only in dreams of unfulfilled desires. A tender atmosphere of expectancy and farewell raises them above palpable momentariness.

In April 1914 Macke made the now rightly famous trip to Tunisia, together with Louis Moilliet and Paul Klee whom he had known since 1911. Within 14 days he produced about 40 aquarelles, a brilliant chain of colourful jewels, in which the " sheer joy of nature " as Macke himself said about them was given shape in its purest form. He was 27 years old and a master. The series is like an illuminated festival of colour. The precision of application, the differentiation of the chromatic scale, the finesse in changing

from saturation point to transparency, are such as would have demanded much meditation. And yet these aquarelles, despite all their precision, have at the same time all the freshness and spontaneity of works created directly in situ. Within the few months that he still had before the outbreak of war he had used up the harvest of the journey.

The African journey also proved a turning point in Paul Klee's artistic development. Up till then he had mainly drawn—strange lemur-like, spectral figurines, similar to Kubin, and swiftly and delicately drawn landscapes. Since 1898 he had been in Munich, studying, among others, with Stuck; previously he had been undecided whether to become a musician or a painter. In 1911 he encountered the *Blaue Reiter* painters; in their second (graphic arts) exhibition he showed seventeen works. Then followed the journey to Kairuan. Referring to the " dark powers " of the African sun he noted: " I am going to stop work now. Deep inside myself I know for certain that colour has caught me... I am a painter."

Paul Klee's work can be compared to a magic microcosm, pregnant with secrets. His nature was as clear as it was tender—friends would say, when he played Mozart it was like a dual revelation—, and his quiet meditative strength was always working to create poetically and pictorially new artistic realities from the different regions of nature and the spirit. These qualities made him one of the most important masters of modern painting. Sincerity and a kind of naive greatness are the characteristics of his best works. These traits may sound somewhat too Victorian and ordinary. But in his art, expressing itself consciously in approximate values, the sincerity is a nationally considered loosening of sentiment, and the naïvité is not that of a child but, almost as if it had been consciously processed, that of a wise man. The poles of his work lie far apart. On the one hand he allows his fantasy to run unchecked to absurdity, and, let it be admitted, to perversity, so that the most reckless artistic acrobatic acts are created; on the other hand his creations condense into profound meditations on undiscovered and unsuspected worlds, or become sinister exclamations about a tragically involved existence, especially in his last works.

At first he occupied a rather peripheral position in the *Blaue Reiter* group, even though he was treated with friendly respect. The African journey, however, did not only transform him into a painter, but the special way in which colour—through Macke's influence—now became the autonomous element of his artistic work, involved him directly in the artistic problems of the group. Their work was all too soon interrupted by the World War. Klee brought his work to maturity alone.

Such titles as *Tapestry of Memories; Full Moon; Villa R.; Movement of Gothic Halls; Waterbirds; Message from an Aerial Spirit;* and gardens, nothing but gardens are the names of the small pictures which he produced until the early twenties. He gives pictorial shape to the nocturnal, the shadowy and the lunar. The drifting sands of memory and sensuous associations form the spiritual basis of his artistic conception which condenses into form in the very act of painting. On the other hand, the picture grows from a primary creative urge which, to begin with, need not necessarily be tied to a given content or form, and which playfully unfolding, first hits upon its " content " in the actual process of creation. " This objective acknowledgment may then perhaps provide the inspiration for this or that addition, which is necessarily related to the formulated object, and for objective accessories which, if the artist is lucky, happen to fit in some place which is still slightly lacking in form, just as if they had always belonged there" (Klee).

In 1921 the artist was appointed to the *Bauhaus* in Weimar. Following the direct lead of Henry van de Velde, Walter Gropius had founded here a modern kind of art school where the ideas of medieval masons' guilds and ideas from the Pedagogic Province in Goethe's *Wilhelm Meister* were combined into a generous synthesis with the ideas of the contemporary reform movements which we have already spoken of. After the collapse of the era of Emperor Wilhelm II the idealists thought the time had come to realize the creation of their " New World." The main ideas were: to bridge the gap which had been brought about between craftsmanship and art during the 19th century, to return to the basic principles of the working and creative processes with respect for the properties of the material, to make use of all the achievements of modern techniques, to reject every kind of imitation, to study the artistic laws, to arouse the creative impulses in the students who by joining a workshop were able to rise from apprentice to journeyman. The aim was that all should work together, each with his own task, subordinate to architecture (Hildebrandt). Lyonel Feininger, Johannes Itten, and Gerhard Marcks joined the foundation in 1919; Adolf Meyer and Georg Muche in 1920, followed early in the next year by Klee; Oskar Schlem-

◁ *Lyonel Feininger* Market Church, Halle, 1930 Oil, 40″× 32″ Bavarian State Collection, Munich

Lyonel Feininger Cyclists, 1912
Oil, 32″ × 40″ Galerie Ferdinand Moeller, Cologne

mer, Kandinsky, and finally Laszlo Moholy-Nagy completed the original faculty. Klee took over first the workshop for painted glass, then the weaving class; Schlemmer was in charge of the workshop for stone sculpture, Feininger ran the printing shop, Kandinsky was in charge of the workshop for mural painting and taught theory. The principles of form as laid down by the *Bauhaus*, and their application to architecture, furniture, domestic utensils, typography, etc., determine still the form of our contemporary surroundings. Painting had to be done " secretly," at least during the first few years; later Klee conducted a painting class. One of the happiest theses of the *Bauhaus* people was that art could neither be taught nor learned. They believed, however, that it was possible to instruct the pupils in the elements of artistic work by letting them experiment and by teaching them to acknowledge the particular laws of their craft. " Modern painting " had become a reality. Kandinsky and Klee made it their aim above all to consolidate their principles by working out the specific dimensions of the pictorial. What, for example, was the relationship between " point and line, and area " (Kandinsky), what were the " dimen-

Otto Dix Portrait of the Poet Theodor Daeubler, 1927
Oil, 59″ × 40″ Haubrich Collection, Wallraf-Richartz Museum, Cologne ▷

Oskar Schlemmer Group at Banister I, 1931 Oil, 36″× 24″ Collection of Ida Bienert, Munich

Karl Hofer Lunares, 1953 Oil, 40″× 30″ State Collection, Karlsruhe

Max Ernst Euclid, 1945
Oil, 24″× 26″   Collection of Jean de Mêsnil, Houston, Texas

Max Ernst Bird Monument, 1927
Oil, 24″× 26½″   Collection of Vicomtesse de Noailles, Paris ▷

Alexander Kanoldt Still Life, 1925
Oil, 21″ × 25″ Kunsthalle, Mannheim

sions " of colour, what determined the quality of material and what pedagogic use could be made of? It was necessary to find a grammar for the new language. It is true that the lesser masters rarely succeeded in progressing further than optical experiments on the fringe of the artistic. But also with Kandinsky and even with Klee, a marked tendency towards coolness, rationality and constructivism can be observed due to the influence of the mainly intellectual climate of the *Bauhaus*. The Expressionism of the *Sturm und Drang* period began to consolidate itself. Pure geometric forms drawn with ruler and compass become more and more frequent with Kandinsky. The abundance of form-combinations, the inexhaustible wealth of variations of simple circular and triangular shapes, the intelligent sensitivity for the direction and strength of line, for its beginning, its interruption, its multiplication in parallels, as well as the clever use of colour, the dialectic of its tones—all these factors make his pictures impressive manifestations of an abstract intelligence, which dogmatically rejects all direct emotion, all " meaning."

Hans Purrmann Flowers, 1914 Oil, 36″ × 29″ Bavarian State Collection, Munich ▷

Oskar Kokoschka Venice, 1924
Oil, 30″× 37″ Bavarian State Collection, Munich

When Kandinsky thought about the spiritual in art he realized that the artist " can no longer manage... with only abstract forms. These forms are too unprecise for him. To limit oneself exclusively to un-precise forms means to limit one's possibilities, to exclude human values and thereby to impoverish one's means of expression."

In view of Kandinsky's later pictures, one is thus brought to the conclusion by his own argumentation that he was there not improbably only concerned with experiments on the potential aesthetic reaction of formal infusoria, or, to put it more exactly: pictorial analysis of the elements of form and colour. The absolute correctness of such a view is weakened by the fact that despite the limitations in expressive power, a new world of form was being created. It is true that the work of art is no longer a totality. But its aesthetic completeness, which it succeeds in preserving, its inherent symmetry and harmony, its well-grounded rejection of everything superficial, and above all its value as a pictorial act of avowal, gives it an enduring artistic importance.

Whereas Kandinsky's pictorial world became rigid under the coercion of being systematized, Klee's works

Oskar Kokoschka Portrait of Mrs. Nancy Cunard, 1924 Oil, 36″× 27″ Collection of Ida Bienert, Munich ▷

retain a warm heart pulse even in the coolest of his formal pictures. His experience with weaving and stained glass introduced him to new forms.

Pure drawing also comes more into its own again during the *Bauhaus* era. Whatever the individual character of his works may be, Klee always starts from the line. All his lines seem to be drawn just as much with conscious intelligence as with intuition. At times one can almost believe that he drew with his left hand in order to deprive the line of some of the rational sureness that would otherwise be given upon it by the right; it would lend it that indigent character, that appearance of being not quite complete which incites the spectator to creative participation. The slight variations from the level that seem to flirt with the horizontal illustrate this characteristic, as do the forms resembling houses, gables, and cupolas, which, by almost imperceptible deviations from the vertical, almost convince one that they can defy their own nature. Equilibrium, although seeming to be constantly threatened, is invariably preserved or created by one last, and sometimes quite delicate, effort.

In the same way that line is closely investigated for its innate creative possibilities, so colour is examined for its powers of artistic expression. By means of the colour circle Klee analyzes colour relationships, the primary colours and their components. " So far as I am able to say from my own experience, it depends on the momentary disposition of the artist to decide which of the many elements should emerge from the general scheme, from their well-regulated position, in order to bring about a new relationship."

In 1925 the *Bauhaus* had to move from Weimar to Dessau as a result of a cultural policy already showing the influence of Nazism. There the old conception deteriorated in the course of time because of internal difficulties. In 1931 Klee accepted an appointment at the Duesseldorf Academy. It was here that the " divisionistic" pictures were created. Directly after his return from Kairuan his colour began winning its independence from the object; the process of emancipation continued at the *Bauhaus*, and, as in the pictures produced after the Egyptian journey, colour had already become an autonomous element of the picture; in fact, it had done more than this: it had become a means of expression in its own right. Its optic and psychic dimensions had provided the realm of a new beauty. In the divisionistic pictures it appears dematerialized, no longer a solid, but a quality of light.

When the horror of National Socialism destroyed the freedom of humanity and the arts in 1933, Klee, returned to Bern, the town of his childhood. The uprooting effects of his emigration had brought about a deep split in his being. Themes like *Demonism*, *The Outbreak of Fear*, *Death and Fire*, began to win the upper hand. It is a heart-rending finale. The blooming, poetic world, illuminated from within, withers; the jewel-like colours run. Instead of his small intricate size Klee now uses a much larger scale. Disparate rudiments of human beings, animals, and plants appear together in the picture, like a disjointed script. These hieroglyphic signs can be shockingly mute or like a piercing shriek, but nearly always one can sense the pervasion of fear, dread, and anguish. The abstract is supplanted by a new figurative style of inner monumentality. *Insula Dulcamara* (1938) seems like an attempt at deliverance from oppression, and many an angel that he painted may have been like a consoling promise for him...

On the invitation of the *Blaue Reiter*, Lyonel Feininger had taken part in the " First German Autumn Exhibition " at Herwarth Walden's in 1913. He was an American of German origin, had been living in Germany since 1887, and had become acquainted with Delaunay in Paris in 1911. His *Cyclists* (1912) owe their form to the latter, who was an important stimulant for modern German painting. But not only to Delaunay. The theme itself has something Futurist about it; the motif of movement in the turning wheels, and the interweaving of the revolving forms with the Cubist element that provide directional crescendo, and the almost audible motory quality of the picture, point to the assimilation of Futurist ideas. This is the exordium of Feininger's personal form of expression, which, limited in its way, nevertheless belongs to the finest achievements of modern form. The broad blue of sea and sky, with the shapes of the sailing boats which he saw as floating domes of light or as airy sea-spirits, combine to form a delicate, transparent consonance of extremely sensitive plane shapes. In addition he painted architectural topics, village churches, gabled houses, cathedrals, and skyscrapers. In all his pictures the objective material has been keenly observed, but is made subordinate to a strict, sensitive scheme and, as a dematerialized realistic form, fused into the organism of the picture. A cleverly and precisely thought-out equipoised structure of lines, which reminds of Klee, forms the frame for his volatile visions. His works, in their translucid ideality, have the effect of irrational reflections. From 1924-1934 (Feininger, too, left Germany, after fourteen years teaching at the *Bauhaus*) he exhibited together with Klee, Kandinsky, and Jawlensky in Germany and America under the name of *Die Blauen Vier*. This was like an echo of the early period.

Lovis Corinth Walchensee, 1924
Oil, 28″× 33″ Bavarian State Collection, Munich

Oskar Schlemmer was one of those painters at the *Bauhaus*—as, by the way, was also Georg Muche—
—who did not belong to the *Blaue Reiter* group. He had studied with Hoelzel in Stuttgart, together
with Willi Baumeister and Otto Meyer-Amden. Schlemmer deferred to the *Bauhaus* program much
more than Kandinsky, Klee, or Feininger, whose pictures were produced almost independently. His
pictures are conscious of their subservient role, they allow themselves to be dominated by architecture,
they have a mural quality. His works were entirely based on the human body, but not on the human
body as an organic natural form; in his pictures it is reduced to its stereometric basic forms. It becomes
the sum of its mechanical functions, a jointed doll. Space is dominated by the figure like a ballet stage
and is not an essential condition, like volume or atmosphere; it is governed and conquered by man.
Schlemmer's ballets sprang from the same ideas, from the same desire for an austere architectonic form.
In the schematic heads, whose contours have been reduced to a bare minimum, there is at times an under-
tone of reticent melancholia.

IV

After the First World War, as after every other catastrophe, hope and desperation arose as antipodal twins out of the destruction. Hope strengthened the *Bauhaus* artists' idealistic belief in the future, desperation gave birth to Surrealism. Surrealism is not a style. At first it was a *Weltanschauung* whose representatives, believing that the suicidal course of civilization had resulted in total bankruptcy, sought new relationships. They considered that conscious exclusion of reasoning, which they thought was reducing itself to absurdity, and the rigorous rejection of logic, would enable new worlds and latent forms of human existence to develop from the inexhaustible springs in the deepest layers of the subconscious and the pregnant region of dreams. The scientific research on, and the artistic representation of " the other side " had actually already been a favourite theme of art and science in the 20th century; the Surrealists, however, hoped that, in a trance-like condition, it would be possible to raise those treasures by the command of their involuntary inner voice, by so-called " psychic automatism." They ironically and grotesquely jeered at everything. Not only reason, but the whole of civilization and culture, art as " creation," the intellect, morals, and all tradition, were robbed of their inherent worth and dignity with macabre joy, they riddled the whole apparently invulnerable accumulation of experience. The declamatory pathos of the Futurists was thus revived. The objective experience of the *Pittura Metafisica*, which, through alienation, had been transposed to inscrutability, made its mark. It was an international movement. In 1913 Kandinsky, in his *Sounds*, had already experimented with alogic verses with nonsensical word patterns; Dada was founded in Zurich in 1916, in 1917 a group was formed in Berlin and in 1919 one in Cologne.

Max Ernst took part in the founding of the Cologne group. He went to Paris in 1922 and stayed in France for many years; later he went to America: a world citizen of German origin. In Paris he joined the Surrealist movement, whose manifesto was formulated by André Breton. Max Ernst is the most important Surrealist painter. He made visible what had up till then only been lived, felt, or written. He painted what the others had only stammered about after their psychic deep-sea dives. He painted pictures that did not claim to be pictures. As he said himself, his object was " to fix the optical hallucination with the utmost precision." The main principle of his abstruse and provocative, and at the same time beautiful and terrible, pictorial world, lay—to quote him again—in the " phenomena discovered by the Surrealists that the juxtaposition of two (or more) apparently alien elements on an alien plane promotes the most potent poetic combustion."

This way the dividing lines between the subjective and objective worlds, between reality and parapsychological vision, are removed. The means of realization are unlimited. Whether the elements originate from 19th-century woodcut illustrations, or whether " unaesthetic " materials are used in contradictory combinations (Kurt Schwitters' " refuse " [Merz] pictures belong to this type), or whether it is that a rubbing from the grain of planks serves as a stimulating fantastic background for hallucinatory powers, the hitherto nonexistent is made visible with playful joy and with contradictory exactitude. The ridiculous, fragmentary and obscene, the vegetable, animal and cosmic—everything is wrenched out of its natural order, raised to the sphere of terror and shock and thereby brought close to the operative region of magic. The mode of representation is exaggeratd at times to a realism delivered with penetrating meticulousness. In Surrealism, the unconscious and the intellectual contracted a clever marriage. Certain elements: a pre-threshold quality, the " super-real," the combinatory, the making visible of organic processes with heterogeneous form fragments—all these characteristics are also exhibited in other painters, for example, in Picasso or Braque, and especially in Paul Klee, without one being able to call them Surrealists.

Magic and reality, however, which occurred in Surrealism as an abstruse alogic compound, appeared on a completely different level in the *Neue Sachlichkeit* (New Objectivity), that phase of modern German painting, which Roh (1925) characterized as " magic realism." We have already spoken of the consolidation of the *Bruecke* style, of that process of taming and stabilization to which painting was subjected in the twenties. We have also mentioned the turn towards constructivism made by the abstract " Expressionists." Schlemmer's treatment of figures might be interpreted in a similar way. Against the turbulent background of a world thrown into confusion by the aftermath of the war, there now began a

Lovis Corinth Ecce Homo, 1925 Oil, 75″× 59″ Museum of Art, Basel ▷

Max Beckmann Cabaña, 1928
Oil, 26″ × 34″   Bavarian State Collection, Munich

period of calm in the arts, which can be observed just as much in Picasso's and Stravinsky's Classicist phases as in the *Valori Plastici* in Italy. In Germany, the realism of Otto Dix should be taken as a protest against the " cosmic ecstasies " of the Expressionists in both camps. There is a touch of " Sunday Painting " about his early works; he also considered the possibilities of Surrealism. Rousseau, *le Douanier*, was his distant guiding star. But then—after the inhuman torment he suffered in the trenches—the mortally wounded soul of the painter hurled itself against war. The pictures are charged with a blazing hatred. He mercilessly paints the shattered bodies and exposes a nauseating, monstrous reality. Without pathos, without sentimentality. But with the cold precision of a machine which registers the last twitches of the skin. Like George Grosz, he also comments satirically on politics and society. The swampy, oily underworld of profiteers and brothels is described with the same bitter veracity. Max Beckmann is a kindred spirit. The power of frank observation is once again cultivated. A new objectivity comes to

Max Beckmann   Self-Portrait, 1944   Oil, 37″ × 24″   Bavarian State Collection, Munich ▷

Max Beckmann Departure, 1932-35
Oil, Center Panel, 85″×45″, Side Panels, 85″× 40″   Museum of Modern Art, New York, N.Y.

the fore, " not the longed for, but the existing world " (Roh) becomes the theme. This also affects the technique: the personal style is replaced by a cool, sober method which can lend the pictures a certain Old Master's smoothness. The portrait of the poet Theodor Daeubler, whose poems (about Franz Marc, for example) and essays (about Expressionist art) helped to interpret modern painting, shows the new objectivity and the new relationship to reality.

One of the main representatives of the New Objectivity, in its narrower sense, is Alexander Kanoldt. He was secretary to the New Artists' Association, and after its dissolution (1912), became one of the charter members of the Munich New Secession, which was formed in the following year. In 1920 he resigned because of the " lack of program " and worked in personal contact with Georg Schrimpf and Karl Mense in Munich. At that time, in addition to architectural paintings, in which he smoothly imposed the stereometric realistic shapes of towering Italian cities on a Cubist principle of form, he created his equipoised still lifes with flowers, jugs, and vases. They are full of challenging objectivity. Even here, however, where reality is consciously sought, he does not feel it to be an objective fact. However much it lacks the emotional expression, it is nevertheless, in its immobility and material density, a subjective composition, not reality imitated, but a new creation and therefore far away from the Naturalism of the 19th century. While rejecting the communicativeness of atmosphere and the charm of a picturesque chiaroscuro, the objects retain a stubborn isolation. Austerely configurated, they remain motionless, as if in transfixed muteness. They possess a strangely timeless constancy, and this very quality enables them to outgrow mere objectivity and win a kind of magical spirituality.

Although Karl Hofer's paintings lack this trait of startling impartiality, one may nevertheless mention him in connection with this group, because of his closeness to nature. He is an individualist. Neither Marées nor Cézanne whom he himself considered his guiding stars, exercised direct creative influence. Hofer is an intelligent and carefully constructive painter, who, in his lyrical figures of girls, his couples at windows, and also in his Italian Ticino landscapes, creates a classical ideality full of subdued nostalgia. At times this harmonious melody is disturbed. Oppressive masquerades, dark accusations of Kafka-like ulteriority (as in *Black Rooms*), or Chagall-like fantasies as in the picture *Lunares*, would suddenly invade his secure domain: the postulate of an unscathed world could not be maintained without inner conflict.

V

Nevertheless there is a kind of modern painting in Germany that does not subject itself to doctrine. We do not mean the many picturemakers who comfortably adopt the vocabulary of their fathers, or even of their grandfathers, nor do we refer to those pictures to which those mildly criticizing words of Goethe may be applied which the German poet wrote about the poetry of his time: " Productions are now being possible which can be nonentities without being bad. Nonentities because they have no content; not

Werner Gilles   Stormy Night, 1948
Oil, 31½″× 40″   Collection of Markus Kruss, Berlin

Ernst Weiers Early Snow, 1953
Oil, 30″ × 37″ Municipal Gallery, Munich

bad, because the authors generally follow the lines of a well accepted pattern." In the originality of their form as well as in their content, the works of Purrmann, but above all the works of Kokoschka and the late works of Corinth, tower above the empty regions of eclecticism. Their painting remains always close to perceptible reality, and therefore its understanding generally causes little difficulty—the importance of modern painting does not lie in its unintelligibility—although it has its own greatness. Only at first sight does it seem quite different from the art of the revolutionaries of the first quarter of the century. Their painting, despite its modernity, clearly remains in the line of tradition. This art does not accept the phrase about the revaluation of all values at face value; the original genius of painting is given expression. Its masters have a sensuous, corporal relationship to colour. This miraculous material is their lifeblood. What dancing means for the southern peoples, fiddle music for the gypsies, so painting is for them a direct and musical means of expression. But even so, these painters think. It is only that their artistic understanding is not of a rational kind. They paint without reflection, they do not measure their work against an idea. It is sufficient in itself, it *is* the idea. This does not mean to say that Expressionism or Abstract painting is " literary," nor that the painting of Corinth or Kokoschka squandered its resources on beautiful craftsmanship. Just as that other kind of painters could be compared with the sentimental poets, so could one also call these naive. Their rejection of the absolute validity of perspec-

Willi Baumeister Eidos V, 1939
Mixed Technique, 40″ × 32″ Bavarian State Collection, Munich

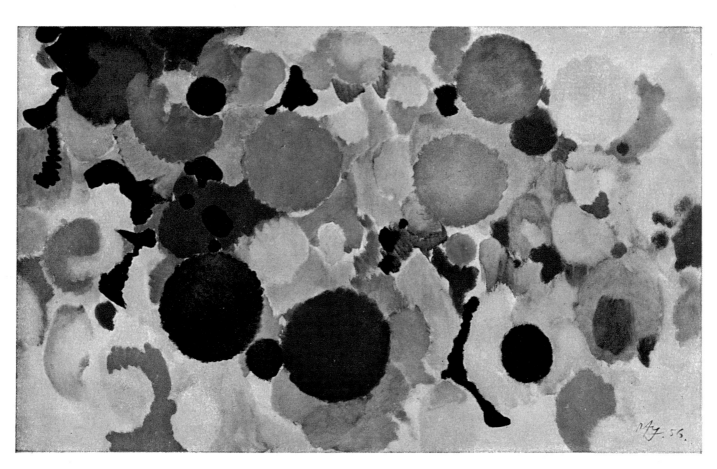

Ernst Wilhelm Nay Chromatic, Strong and Tender, 1956
Oil, 50″× 80″ Private Collection

Fritz Winter Great Finale, 1952
Oil, 37″× 63″ Kunsthalle, Mannheim

tive, their emancipation of colour from the object, their directness of expression and also their form, make them living witnesses of contemporary art. The present has many faces. The differences lie in the type. To quote Schiller: " The value of the one lies in his absolute achievement of finite greatness, of the other in his approach to infinite greatness." United though they are in opposing the Expressionists and Abstract art, and despite all their similarity in their relationship to their medium, how they vary!

Hans Purrmann went to Paris in 1905 after having studied with Stuck in Munich for a number of years. He wanted to see paintings by Manet and discovered Matisse. In the latter, he did not only find the painter who was to determine his artistic development, but also a friend. From 1909 until the outbreak of the First World War he worked as " *massier* " (shop steward) at Matisse's school. In the *Café du Dôme* he met like-minded friends: Weisgerber, Hugo Levy, Ahlers-Hestermann; later Oskar Moll joined them. Purrmann may serve here as representative of this group. He, like the others, did not follow the decorative flat style which the Fauves had developed under Matisse's leadership, but Matisse's bright, luminous colourfulness was nevertheless a pattern for all of them. Also the way in which the colour in Purrmann's resplendent interiors and still lifes is sensuously spread and combined to form fine, well-balanced harmonies may be attributed to his friendship with Matisse. Purrmann's discursive, caressing brush stroke, however, the maintenance of a discretely interwoven colour ensemble, and the charming sweetness of his colour chords, bring him occasionally close to Renoir. Purrmann is a *causeur* in whom wisdom and *esprit* are combined in a rare fashion. His pictures reflect his *joie de vivre*. They are like witty incidental music.

Oskar Kokoschka is an Austrian. The Vienna of Sigmund Freud, Karl Kraus, and Peter Altenberg gave shape to the painter's particular kind of vibrant intellect and psychic high tension. The symbolistic, precious selectivity of *Art Nouveau* as practiced by Gustav Klimt at the *Wiener Werkstaetten*, is the distinguishing feature of his artistic exordium. *The Dreaming Boys*, a symbolistic fairy tale of sentimental sexuality and delicate fragility of form, is his first poetic graphic work. Adolf Loos, the teacher of forms of a new, anti-ornamental style in Austria, helped the young Kokoschka by getting him commissions for portraits. Those early portraits of the years 1908-1910 were branded by contemporary critics as " shameless revelations." Certainly they were anything but drawing-room likenesses. With almost mediumistic intuition for the sitter's psyche behind his visual appearance, the eye of the painter penetrates the surface, skins his " victims " and projects his own inner image with hallucinatory sureness on the canvas. That is Expressionism, except for the form which, as such, is without direct preliminary stages. Egon Schiele and Richard Gerstl, both short-lived geniuses, were kindred spirits, who burst the bonds of *Art Nouveau* and academism by the furiousness of a kind of emotional painting. With Kokoschka, the nervous line, which twines itself into knots and coils, and which here and there concentrates into polypean fossils of spiritual excitement, is combined with a darkly blended colourfulness. From 1910 on he contributed regularly to the *Sturm*. In the years 1913-1914 his colours gain both in substance and concentration. With explosive vehemence they are applied with the finger or a knife, rarely with the brush, in greasy, slippery layers. These are orgies of expression. The first landscapes were painted in Switzerland in 1910; like his portraits, they are impulsive visions, which reflect the painter's spiritual development. With exhibitionist movements he reveals in his works the erotic stages and macabre experiences of his hectic existence. After the Dresden period (1917-1924) his colours became progressively lighter and more effervescent. Up to the very brink of libertinism the pulse of the hand determines with reflexive directness the structure of the composition. His highly differentiating visual ability, the spontaneity of his colours, but above all his special sensibility, fuse and create in the landscapes seen with his intoxicated vision, poetic images of metaphysical transparency. It is always the miracle of the vis-à-vis, the other, the counter-ego, which he penetrates questioning with a morbid, self-destroying devotion —as a little boy he once took a burning coal out of the fire. His painting is a kind of self-redemption which bravely accepts the risk of failure.

Kokoschka's mature works have been characterized as " dramatic Impressionism," but this phrase seems far more applicable to the late works of Lovis Corinth. For despite the fierceness of the colour vibrations, Kokoschka's colours are not developed from the object, but from the painter's subjective impression. With Corinth on the other hand, the relation to the object always remains unequivocal, despite the high degree of dramatization. The ageing master underwent one of the deepest changes ever experienced by any of the German modern painters. In 1911, at the age of 53, Corinth who shared with Liebermann and Slevogt the leading position among the German Impressionists, suffered a stroke. Up to that time, out of the fullness of his happy, powerful nature, the artist had created a type of painting

Georg Meistermann Tearing Up, 1953
Oil, 60″× 80″ Private Collection

glowing with sensuous passion. However, this experience with death awakened other powers in Corinth. A most touching change of style took place. As if in an attempt to cheat the threatening death of another work with a last effort, his painting takes on a certain velocity. The surface is torn, and at first it seems as if the delectably replete brush strokes of Manet have been combined with the composition of Cézanne (1913). But soon they lose all their cultivation, all their acquired control and bend themselves to an all-powerful law, as if driven by a stormwind. The heavens collapse, buildings totter, faces resemble a land-scape deranged by a hurricane. The Walchensee pictures produced after 1917 are like a passionate ritor-nello, the series of self-portraits like a dance of death. It was German Expressionism, it was Oskar Ko-koschka, who evoked Corinth's expressive power and freed his form language of its Impressionistic fetters. One of his last works was the moving *Ecce Homo*, painted in 1925, the year of his death. Unless one feels that the assistant figures were arbitrarily chosen, it seems as if war and laboratorial science deliver humanity to the cross...

" Let us go on living, let us go on, like miners in a dark pit, but with a bright lamp that throws its light into deep shafts and whose light consists of two elements, faith and consciousness," as was written by Max Beckmann, the great apocalyptist of our time. He found himself amidst the contradictory currents of modern painting. He crossed blades with Franz Marc. He saw the social and political chaos with wide-awake eyes, and was himself caught up in it—his emigration was not the first effect it had on him—and he recognized the threat to humanity that was growing to monstrous proportions. With a tremendous independence he created his own laws—against all the reigning tendencies and doctrines.

His topic is man. His *Great Death Scene* (1906), which was painted in the style of the Berlin Secession made Munch interested in him. In 1910 he painted the Messina earthquake on a giant canvas, and in

1912, the *Titanic* disaster, also on an enormous scale. He felt the undisguised reality of the war to be the " gloomy salutations of eternity," and was later to paint it as such. In 1917 his own style begins to take shape. In the pictures from the following years appear groups of bestial people, cramped together as if in shelters without exits. The individual being is cruelly isolated. Trumpet, candle, fish—puzzling ciphers—connect as if accidentally the crowded figures in the heartless lumber of the picture space. The uglified proletarian grimaces are drawn with poisonous precision. Beckmann's closeness to Otto Dix and George Grosz is evident, though he does not use such detailed drawing. And however much they may agree in their indictment of everything established, Beckmann's work nevertheless dispenses with provocative criticism. It is not caustic disintegration, but the transfixing of chaos by the tyranny of his form. His pictures do not practice social criticism, they are rather the artistic manifestation of a definite form of human existence.

Compared with these paintings, which are distinguished by a strange transparency colour, the works he produced towards the middle of the twenties achieve a powerful tension, a cold passion, also in their colour. A picture like *Cabaña* creates a new reality. " My constant aim is to capture the magic of the so-called reality, and to translate this reality into painting—to make the invisible visible through reality." And Beckmann himself added: " It may sound paradoxical, but it is actually reality that forms the secret of our existence." This, however, does not give expression to objective experience as understood by the New Objectivity; this is a basically quite different reaction to the objectivity of reality. " My dream, for example, is... to transform the optical impression of the objective world by an inner transcendental arithmetic." This means, however, that Beckmann, despite the complete difference of form, and despite all his outspoken antagonism, was an Expressionist in his creative processes. And when he defined his painting as " experiencing existence," and said " to be conscious of oneself more and more, that is after all the whole idea of art," that was also an admission in the same sense.

During the years from 1932 to 1935 the first of Beckmann's great triptych paintings was created, *Departure (Abfahrt)*. " It is not difficult to interpret what was painted in the years from 1932 to 1935 by a man martyred by his nerves under the very significant title *Scenes from Shakespeare's Tempest;* with a cipher language of his own creation he once again shook at the dying era. It was not difficult for him, because the *unum necessarium*, the basic condition of spiritual life, never burned stronger in the soul of the sufferer. There was raging force, both without and within; without, brutality, the executioner's henchman; within, the prisoners of the deranged senses. Only the spiritually great are able to free themselves of such dark powers: a prince turns his back on the horrors. Another mysterious, benevolent Charon, this time in the bright light of midday, rows towards an unknown shore. Silent and solemn, the woman stands in the mythical boat, carrying a child, the pledge of the gods, at her breast. What is being saved? Perhaps that tenderness that was given to the painter at the outset. In the meantime the water flows, and driven by unseen sails of hope, with idle oars, a noble freight is carried to infinity " (Reifenberg).

Further triptychs were created, sometimes using old topics in new forms, as, for example, *Actors, Acrobats, Carnival*. The climax of his work are the triptychs on mythological themes. Beckmann's attitude towards the Greek myths is the same as his attitude towards reality: both are absorbed with all the strength of his soul and his intellect, then recast in the smeltery of his own heart and thoughts, and condensed into a new personal shape. His figures in these triptychs are monumental in their classical greatness. The majestic personages, later also against a background of sea and sky, have a statuesque impressiveness, presaging songs of deep mourning. Contemporaneous commonplaceness seems to have been withdrawn here to the same degree as the remoteness of mythical past has been advanced and given corporeality—disenchantment and enchantment in one.

The Amsterdam self-portrait (1944), one of many that Beckmann painted throughout his life, is probably the most moving portrait of our time. Here we are faced with humanity—calling out and demanding answer—in all its greatness, as an integral part of modern painting; to use Beckmann's own words, " this humanity, with the expression of want and abandonment and yet with the power and quiet dignity of immutability."

VI

People, however, who were conscious of their existential want and abandonment, who seriously wanted " truth," and sought to give shape to their ideas in freedom, such people could not be employed as soldiers. For that, " heroes " were needed to wield their arms cruelly and stupidly for apparent ideals, unweakened by feelings or thoughts. And so the cultural powers of the Hitler regime declared men like Beckmann and Klee, actually all the painters dealt with here, to be "degenerate." They were dismissed from their posts, their pictures were confiscated from museums, they were forbidden to exhibit, or even to work, and at the same time their works were sold abroad to bring in currency. Art became a means of "people's education," was degraded to the status of a propaganda puppet. A kind of sentimental-heroic art was encouraged, which was just on the right intellectual level for the "little man." The great masters, however, had to leave Germany or go into hiding. Some of them continued to work in secrecy. Only in a few places, at the art dealer Guenther Franke's in Munich, or in the Buchholz Gallery in Berlin, for example, was it possible to see modern painting. Their secret cupboards were only opened, it is true, for "good" people.

Apart from the brutal effects of the political machinery of National Socialism, which do not need to be detailed here, there was a quasi-intellectual element behind the battle against the so-called "decadent art" which unites all those *Weltanschauungen* and institutions which count on man as being an ascertainable quantity, or, to be more accurate, have to count on his being so, if they want to retain their position of power. New, deep, and astonishing, delightful and dangerous aspects of mankind had been given shape in the artistic work of the Moderns. This phenomenon possessed the incendiary power of the revolutionary. It bore the hallmark of utmost honesty. It withdrew from the orthodox canon of beauty. And what was given expression in it about mankind burst the bounds of what had up till then been accepted as the standard categorization. This also explains the militant antagonism which it still encounters today from various sides; the battle has more than just a political aspect, and naturally it is not of only an "aesthetic" quality. The reason for this must be sought in the very nature of this kind of art. It flees the aesthetic. It manifests an attitude towards life, it strives to provoke recognition (although it can naturally not bring about an act of recognition in its strict sense); as an "avowal," however, as an evaluation, as a philosophy of world and man, it transcends today—just as it did at the beginning—the carefully protected little garden of the merely artistic. Therein lies its greatness. Therein lies its dangerousness as well as its danger.

Franz Marc said: "Art is no longer there to serve man as a more or less important pretext." These "pretexts" have actually gone; nevertheless there are still ties which are prescribed by the rigorous conscientiousness of the artist. In its s e r i o u s n e s s, which s t r i v e s f o r t r u t h, in its c o u r a g e and in its f r e e d o m—those are the virtues that are demanded by the contemporary theologian and philosopher, Romano Guardini, from the man of the future—it has its own ethos, which, however, is not derived from a blindly accepted dogma. If it is true—as Werner Heisenberg says—that man on this earth, for the first time in history, is faced only by himself, then this does not only apply to the natural philosophy of contemporary physics, but also to the whole of the spiritual and intellectual existence of man. That does not exclude an orientation towards metaphysical religious powers. Questionable though its merits are, one must nevertheless consider the art of our time, for that very reason, as an attempt at reorientation, as a way, as a possibility of finding one's own place in the fundamentally altered life into which we have been born. For art today it is more difficult than ever before to provide a universally valid answer. This is not only due to the changed sociological role of the work of art, nor only to the different relationship between the spectator and the work; the artist himself has a very critical attitude towards his own production. "There is much semblance in a work, one could go further and say that it is semblant in itself, as ' work '..., and one asks oneself, whether, at the present state of our consciousness, of our knowledge, and of our sense of truth, this game is still permissible, still intellectually possible, still to be taken seriously; whether the work as such, the self-sufficient and harmoniously balanced creation, still has any legitimate relation to the utter insecurity, to the problematic situation and lack of harmony of our social condition; whether not all semblance, even the most beautiful, and especially the most beautiful, has turned into a l i e" (Thomas Mann). *Honi soit qui mal y pense!* Or even wrests this weapon out of the artist's hand and turns it against him.

Art can no longer be taken for granted. No more than any other form of communication between men can be. But it is there. And it must be taken seriously wherever—consciously or unconsciously— it grows out of the middle of this, our very existence, and does not build threadbare altars out of the ruins of memory.

This is no question of style. The alternatives of "great abstract or great concrete," which are now presented by the art critics, are, in our opinion, a logical bottleneck derived from artistic dogma, considering the artistic possibilities of modern painting as a whole. Picasso, one of the greatest painters of our time, stands midway between these extremes, just as are Klee and Beckmann. With regard to a future synthesis of the " purely artistic " and the " objective," Kandinsky said in the *Blaue Reiter:* " The representational forms which were torn out of painting's treasure vault by the intellect can easily be arranged between two poles—on the one hand, complete abstraction, on the other hand, complete realism." And he went on: " These two poles open up two paths, which finally lead to one goal..."

The collapse in 1945 bore the promise of freedom. What had been held in bondage now appeared free again. How could the broken threads be joined? Expressionism had already passed through its final phase in the twenties; the New Objectivity had been carried to absurdity by the platitudinarian naturalism of the National Socialist era. Klee was dead, Kokoschka was in London, and Beckmann in America. Many of the younger ones had been killed in action or had to spend many fruitless years in prisoner-of-war camps. The first surveys of the creative work in Germany during the postwar years showed quite clearly that most of the talented were devoting themselves to Abstract painting. After the years of suppression, the most extreme direction appeared the most fruitful. Out of the belief and hope of the utterly impoverished and against the background of a cruelly ravaged environment, the younger generation created signs which they were able to believe would provide those " symbols of the future intellectual religion " of which Franz Marc had spoken. But it happened that these symbols did not exist, that the signs were only ciphers for something inexpressible—as Kandinsky had said: they spoke secretively of secrets.

Willy Baumeister had already completely devoted himself to Abstract painting in 1936, not as a continuation of Kandinsky's inventions, but based on the volatile island-like pictures of Arp. He had begun his studies with Hoelzel, but his own style developed first through contact with Ozenfant, with Le Corbusier, and above all with Fernand Léger. His sports pictures of the years 1924-1929 show that same cool constructional and mechanical quality that makes the works of Léger and Baumeister seem less like " paintings " than architectural murals. Baumeister—*nomen est omen* (*Baumeister*, in German, means builder)—had a natural affinity to the wall; it was an accepted basis for his work, not in the way that it is for a born fresco painter, but from the craftsman's point of view. This had already become quite obvious in the " wall pictures " proper (1919-1922): they were reliefs rather than paintings. But again and again, as, for instance, in the " sand pictures " he felt an urge to amalgamate plastic and mural elements. Seen from this angle it is understandable that his work have a certain decorative " ornamental " quality, and at the same time there is something robust and healthy about them. The " Unknown in Art," on which he wrote a book, and which he considered to be his special theme (particularly in his Abstract period), was not a transcendental something which was to be expressed through his work, but it was—quite simply—something never before seen which, based on alien and forgotten elements of Mexican or Egyptian origin, is raised from the sphere of the unknown with playful joy (and a dash of peasant cunning) and inserted in his works as a new abstract form in the guise of the " unknown."

The Non-Objective painting of today is at times only a vibration of the nerves, as Kandinsky oracularly feared; it can be nothing more than an act of dis-inhibition, a psychogrammatical stammering. Its aesthetic integrity remains nevertheless undoubted. With Objective art there is the danger that it appears as a derivative of something now extinct, and that its " beauty " might be considered untrue because the conditions from which it arises are no longer valid. The remote and the past, the alien and the ancient, are today within fascinatingly easy reach. Clever ubiquity shamelessly usurps these spheres. But also the uninitiated, naively participating, wise without knowledge, can partake of these springs.

Werner Gilles worked at the *Bauhaus* in Feininger's class, but he matures slowly and owes his style to no particular school. Klee and Picasso, and also Chagall to a certain degree, are his guiding stars.

Gilles's landscapes, especially his watercolors from Ischia, exude happiness like a folksong set by Bartòk. They are the expression of his existential consciousness based on a deep trust, a *joie de vivre*, which springs from an almost boyish faith. In contrast to the landscapes there are the series of pictures from the world of literature and from classical mythology and legends: the cycles *Ophelia; Dedicated to Arthur Rimbaud; Orpheus; Human and All-Too-Human; Tibetan Deathbook;* and sketches and pictures in which he invokes the poetic element of Mallarmé or Baudelaire, and, time and again, of Hoelderlin, who has the closest affinity to his Greek soul. Fundamental human attitudes, Orphic sounds, holy figures from literature, from strange cults and remote spiritual spheres, are brought into the pictorial present. History is not learning or archetype for Gilles, but a timeless spiritual emotion; an almost " a-perspective " relationship puts him in harmony with those forces whose existential power and presence are evoked in his works. Ernst Weiers, who studied with Klee and Campendonk, is a painter of the younger generation; like

Gilles, he is poised between objectivity and abstraction. He very nearly dispenses, however, with the human figure, which in Gilles's work frequently occurs as the focal point drawn in figurate cryptography. Flowers and trees, the animals of the forest, spiders, owls and toads, cocks and foxes, and birds, living their lives of treacherous bellicosity in the undergrowth, beautiful and malicious—these are the elements of the iridescent world of his pictures, where every detail is observed with the unsentimental eye of the hunter. The artistic form develops from nature. The elliptic shapes of fishes, or the interwoven pattern of flamingo necks, those are the forms used to create a sinuous arabesque as the dominant feature of the picture. Out of the cumbersome contours of weathered firs and jagged mountains, out of the provocative contrast of white snowfields and gleaming red mountain tops, grows the artistic reaction to nature's message: *Early Snow*.

Winter, Nay, and Meistermann are at the time of writing considered the leading exponents of Non-Objective painting in Germany. They differ widely from one another. Meistermann, in his rationality and in his combinatory use of aggressive, polished forms, is related in a way to the late Kandinsky. He seems potentially strongest in his stained glass windows and in works with a specified theme like the large fresco in St. Alphonse's Church, near Wuerzburg. The re-transposition of the pictorial elements of "absolute" painting into an intelligible form language opens up new fields for him. This way the religious content matter whose complete realization through the human figure has apparently not been easily attainable since the 19th century is again expressible. The reprise of Abstract painting after 1945 was not the result of a desire for restoration, which had its effect in only too many spheres in Germany. The formal principle of design, Paul Klee's method of "pictorial thought," holds a canonical validity for the younger generation, and no higher artistic law could be imagined today. However, his artistic work, in its personal brilliance which, even where he is purely abstract, is still thematically tied and suffused with a tragedy that demands participation even in the abstrusely cryptic duologues with the powers of good and evil of the other world; this individual quality defied all conformity or textbook definition. Kandinsky's abstractions, on the other hand, which consciously remain within the dispersonalized, almost "dissouled" colour and form complexes, expert—in their capacity as a kind of experimental theory concerning the harmony of absolute painting— a wider influence. But even his art—as a doctrine and because of that very fact—is still a duologue. The most important characteristic of the Non-Objective art of the younger generation throughout the world which distinguishes it from that of the previous generation seems, however, to be its monological character. It is essentially no longer communication, but contents itself, smug and exclusive, with the arbitrary formation of suggestive creations.

Fritz Winter went to the *Bauhaus* from the mines. His early works recall mineral formations: inclined stratifications, shafts of light, sombre radiations, crystalline refractions—the whole forming a strange, unreal substantiality. Gloomy tones suffuse even the works of the last few years, in which mainly black figurations, executed with a broad brush, carry the composition. They are like coarsened Oriental letters. Behind and between them, quiet colours may passionately glow. As against the unrhetorical static in Kandinsky's late works, and against Klee's final figurate style, a kind of lyrical pathos discloses itself. Traces of an Expressionist inheritance haunt the emotional diction. Man and nature as stimulus or motif are rejected. But it is neither the unconscious nor the psychic that here, in wild brush strokes, desolately revolves about itself; the motory quality of the physical expresses itself—as signature—with the powerful vehemence of a painter who fundamentally is a sentimental romantic.

Ernst Wilhelm Nay's development, from the beginning with Hofer, to the "chromatic" harmonies with brilliantly coloured circles which he now paints, could well be described as a path to loneliness, or, more accurately, to isolation. He fought his way with fiery perseverance, with embittered rigorousness. Like a berserker, he always turned his back on each goal immediately after it had been reached, continually summoning up new energy, in order to wrench something never yet seen into the light. Picasso soon began to influence him. Later, in his Lofoten Islands pictures, which, with the support of Edvard Munch, Nay was able to paint in Norway, figure and landscape interlock to form ringing crystal shapes. Colour retreats and thickens to a lunar yellow. Starting with the small landscape water colors which he did as a soldier in Brittany, and in which natural, earthy, and warm tones predominate, colour becomes more and more the central problem of his work, till it finally, via the erotic dragonfly figurations, develops into the "chromatic" structure of colour-tensions in the circling colour balloons of today. These pictures are no longer "abstractions," but, as free rhythmic colour-harmonies, they pendulate their peculiar powers against and with one another in mutable dialectic. A terminal seems to have been reached.

76

DOCUMENTS

PROCLAMATION OF THE ARTISTS' COMMUNITY OF THE BRUECKE, BY E. L. KIRCHNER, about 1905. From: *Chronik der KG Bruecke*, 1913.

With the belief in a development, in a new generation of creators as well as beholders, we call upon youth to rally, and to win elbow room and the right to live our own lives away from the established older artists. All those belong to us who mirror, direct and unadulterated, that which impels them to create.

THE HISTORY OF THE BRUECKE, BY E. L. KIRCHNER From: *Chronik der KG Bruecke*, 1913.

The painters Bleyl and Kirchner met in Dresden in 1902. Heckel was introduced through his brother, a friend of Kirchner's. Heckel brought with him Schmidt-Rottluff, whom he knew from Chemnitz. They all met in Kirchner's studio in order to work. There it was possible to study the nude, the basis of all the fine arts, in complete freedom. The drawing on this basis resulted in a feeling, which they all shared, that they should extract the stimulus for their work from life and subject themselves to experience. In the book *Odi Profanum*, they each drew and wrote down their own ideas, thereby comparing their individuality. Thus they quite naturally became a group which was given the name *Bruecke* (Bridge). Each provided a stimulus for the other. Kirchner contributed the woodcut from Southern Germany which he had taken up again, inspired by the old woodcuts in Nuremberg. Heckel revived woodcarving again; Kirchner enriched this technique in his own carvings by coloring them, and tried to find the rhythm of the closed form in stone and pewter. Schmidt-Rottluff made the first lithographs directly on the stone. The group's first exhibition took place in their own rooms in Dresden: it won no recognition. Dresden, however, provided plenty of inspiration through the charm of its landscape and its old culture. Here the *Bruecke* artists also found their first footholds in the history of art in Cranach, Beham and other German (late) medieval masters. After an exhibition of his works in Dresden Amiet was elected a member of the *Bruecke*. He was followed in 1905 by Nolde, whose fantastic individuality introduced a new aspect to the *Bruecke*. He enriched our exhibitions by the interesting technique of his etchings, and was introduced to our technique of woodcuts. On his invitation Schmidt-Rottluff joined him in Alsen. Later on Schmidt-Rottluff and Heckel went to Dangast. The keen air of the North Sea gave rise to a monumental form of Impressionism, especially in Schmidt-Rottluff. During this time Kirchner pursued his research work on the closed composition in Dresden: in the negro plastic art and in the beam carvings of the South Seas in the ethnographical museum, he found a parallel to his own creations. Pechstein, in his efforts to free himself from academic sterility, joined the *Bruecke*. Kirchner and Pechstein went to Gelmeroda to work together. The exhibition of the *Bruecke*, with the new members, took place in Richter's Salon in Dresden. The show had a great effect on the young artists in Dresden. Heckel and Kirchner tried to bring new paint-

ing into harmony with space. Kirchner furnished his rooms with murals and batiks which he had painted with Heckel's help. In 1907 Nolde resigned from the *Bruecke*. Heckel and Kirchner went to the Moritzburg Lakes to study the nude in the open air. Schmidt-Rottluff worked towards the perfection of his colour rhythms in Dangast. Heckel went to Italy and brought back with him the stimulus of Etruscan art. Pechstein went to Berlin to carry out some decorative commissions. He tried to introduce the new painting into the Secession. Kirchner took up hand printed lithographs in Dresden. Bleyl, who had turned to teaching, resigned from the *Bruecke* in 1909. Pechstein went to Heckel in Dangast. In the same year both of them joined Kirchner in Moritzburg to paint nudes by the lakes. In 1910 the founding of the "New Secession" was provoked by the rejection of the younger German painters by the old Secession. In order to support Pechstein's position in the New Secession, Heckel, Kirchner, and Schmidt-Rottluff also joined. They met Mueller at the first exhibition of the N. S. In his studio they found a Venus by Cranach, which they also greatly admired. The sensuous harmony between Mueller's life and work made him a natural candidate for membership of the *Bruecke*. He brought to us the charm of size and colour. In order to preserve the purity of the *Bruecke* aims, the members of the *Bruecke* resigned from the New Secession. They came to a mutual understanding only to exhibit jointly in the Berlin "Secession." Then followed an exhibition of the *Bruecke*, occupying all the rooms of the Gurlitt Gallery. Pechstein violated the understanding, became a member of the Secession and was blackballed by the group. The *Sonderbund* invited the *Bruecke* to its exhibition in Cologne in 1912, and commissioned Heckel and Kirchner to decorate its chapel. The majority of the *Bruecke* members now live in Berlin. The *Bruecke* has preserved its internal character here as well. Inwardly integrated, it radiates its new working values into the modern artistic life in Germany. Not influenced by contemporary trends—Cubism, Futurism, etc.— the *Bruecke* has fought for a new culture of man as the basis of true art. The *Bruecke* owes its status in the world of art today to these aims.

WASSILY KANDINSKY: "DER BLAUE REITER" (Reflections) From: *Das Kunstblatt*, 14th year, 1930, p. 57.

Dear Herr Westheim.
You have asked me for my recollections of the founding of the *Blaue Reiter*.
Today—after so many years—this wish is justified, and I am glad to be able to fulfill it.
Today—after so many years—the intellectual atmosphere in Munich—so beautiful, and despite everything so dear—has fundamentally changed. Schwabing, then so noisy and turbulent, has become silent—not a single sound can be heard from there. It is a pity for beautiful Munich, and a still greater pity for the somewhat strange, rather eccentric and self-confident Schwabing, in whose streets a person—whether man or woman (a "*Weibsbuild*")—without palette, or without

canvas, or without at least a portfolio, immediately attracted attention. Just like a "stranger" in a village. Everybody painted—or wrote poetry, or composed music, or danced. In every house there were at least two studios, and even if there was not always a great deal of painting done, a great deal of discussion, disputation, philosophizing, and drinking went on (this last being more dependent on the purse than on moral outlook).

"What is Schwabing?" a Berliner once asked in Munich. "It is a northern district of the town," said a citizen of Munich.

"Certainly not," said another, "it is a spiritual condition." This was nearer to the truth.

Schwabing was a spiritual island in the great world, in Germany, but chiefly in Munich itself.

I lived there for many years. It was there that I painted my first abstract painting. It was there that I mused on "pure" painting, on pure art. I tried to think analytically, to discover synthetic relationships, dreamed of the "great synthesis" that was to come, felt urged to convey my thoughts not only to the island surrounding me, but to the man outside this island. I considered them fecund and necessary.

Thus out of my sketchy notes *pro domo sua* grew my first book *On the Spiritual in Art*. In 1910 it was completed, lying in a drawer, since not a single publisher had the courage to risk the publishing costs (which were low enough, after all). Even the very warm interest that the famous Hugo von Tschudi took in it was of no avail.

At this time my wish to get out a book, a kind of almanac, to which only artists should contribute articles began to take shape. I had mainly painters and musicians in mind. The corruptive separation of one art from another, and furthermore of "art" from folk art and children's art, from "ethnography," the firmly established walls between what I considered to be related or even identical manifestations, in a word, the synthetic relationships, gave me no peace. Today it may well appear strange that for a long time I could find no helpers, no means, simply not enough interest for this idea.

This was the time when so many "isms" were beginning to take shape, the time that was unconscious of synthetic sensibility, and whose main interest was directed towards temperamental "civil wars."

Almost in a day (1911-12) two great styles of painting came into the world: Cubism and Abstract (=Absolute) painting. At the same time Futurism, Dadaism, and the soon triumphant Expressionism were born. Those were hectic times!

Atonal music, and its then universally booed exponent Arnold Schoenberg, excited the emotions no less than the "isms" in painting already mentioned.

I met Schoenberg at that time and immediately found in him an enthusiastic supporter of the *Blaue Reiter* idea. (Our contact was, at the time, limited to correspondence, personal acquaintance followed somewhat later.)

I was already in contact with a few eventual contributors. It was the *Blaue Reiter* of the future, still without any chance of realization.

And then F r a n z M a r c arrived from Sindelsdorf.

One discussion was sufficient: we understood one another completely. I found in this unforgettable man a then most unusual type of artist (is it less unusual today?) who could see far beyond parochialism and who was not so much outwardly as inwardly opposed to hampering, inhibiting traditions.

The publication of "On the Spiritual in Art" by R. Piper I owed to Franz Marc: he paved the way.

For long days and evenings, and now and then late into the night, we discussed our plans. It was crystal-clear to both of us from the beginning that we should have to be strictly dictatorial: complete freedom for the realization of the idea. Franz Marc brought with him the very young A u g u s t M a c k e, an enthusiastic helper. We assigned to him the task of collecting mainly the ethnographical material, and helped him in this. He carried out his job brilliantly, and was then asked to contribute an article on masks, which he did with equal brilliance.

I took care of the Russians (painters, composers, and theoreticians), and translated their articles.

Marc brought a great deal of material back with him from Berlin—it originated from the *Bruecke* which was just being formed and which was completely unknown in Munich.

"Artist, create, don't talk!" This was the reply of some artists who refused our request to contribute articles. That, however, belonged to the negative chapter of refusals, antagonism, and outrage, which shall here remain unsung.

It was urgent! Even before the publication of the book Franz Marc and I organized the first exhibition of the *Redaktion des Blauen Reiters* [1]) in the Thannhauser Gallery—the basis being the same as that of the almanac: no propagation of a definite, exclusive "direction," the presentation of the most diverse manifestations of the new painting on an international basis and—dictatorship. "... how the i n w a r d d e s i r e of the artists manifests itself," I wrote in the preface.

The second (and last) exhibition was one of graphic art in the newly opened Hans Goltz Gallery; about two years ago, shortly before his death, Goltz wrote to me with great enthusiasm about that wonderful time.

My neighbour in Schwabing was P a u l K l e e. He was then still very "small." With justifiable pride, however, I can claim that I already sensed his future greatness in his then quite small drawings (he hadn't yet started to paint). A drawing of his may be found in the *Blaue Reiter*.

I should mention also Franz Marc's extremely generous patron, B e r n h a r d t K o e h l e r. Without his helping hand, the *Blaue Reiter* would have remained a beautiful Utopia, as would Herwarth Walden's "First German Autumn Salon," and many other things.

I planned to juxtapose art and science in the next volume of the *Blaue Reiter*: origin, development of working methods, purpose. Today I am even more conscious than I was then of how many smaller roots lead back to a single large one —work for the future.

But then came the war and swamped these modest plans with everything else.

What is—inwardly!—essential, however, can be postponed, but can not be torn out by the roots.

With best wishes,

Yours,
KANDINSKY

KANDINSKY: CONCERNING THE SPIRITUAL IN ART
Munich, 1912.

Only just now awakening after years of materialism, our soul is infected with the despair born of unbelief, of lack of purpose and aim. The nightmare of materialism, which turned life into an evil, senseless game, is not yet passed; it still darkens the awakening soul. Only a feeble light glimmers, a

---

[1]) We invented the name *Der Blaue Reiter* while sitting around the coffee table in the bower at Sindelsdorf: we both loved blue, Marc as to horses, and I as to riders. Thus the name originated naturally. And Mrs. Maria Marc's wonderful coffee then tasted even better.

tiny point in an immense circle of darkness. This light is but a presentiment; and the mind, seeing it, trembles in doubt over whether the light is a dream and the surrounding darkness indeed reality. This doubt and the oppression of materialism separate us sharply from primitives. Our soul rings cracked when we sound it, like a precious vase, dug out of the earth, which has a flaw. For this reason, the primitive phase through which we are now passing, in its present derivative form, must be short-lived.

The two kinds of resemblance between the forms of art of today and of the past can be easily recognized as diametrically opposed. The first, since it is external, has no future. The second, being internal, contains the seed of the future. After a period of materialistic temptation, to which the soul almost succumbed, and which it was able to shake off, the soul is emerging, refined by struggle and suffering. Cruder emotions, like fear, joy and grief, which belonged to this time of trial, will not longer attract the artist. He will attempt to arouse more refined emotions, as yet unnamed. Just as he will live a complicated and subtle life, so his work will give to those observers capable of feeling them emotions subtle beyond words.

The observer of today is seldom capable of feeling such vibrations. He seeks instead an imitation of nature with a practical function (for example, a portrait, in the ordinary sense) or an intuition of nature involving a certain interpretation (e. g., " impressionist " painting) or an inner feeling expressed by nature's forms (as we say, a picture of " mood ").[1] When they are true works of art, such forms fulfill their purposes and nourish the spirit. Though this remark applies to the first case, it applies more strongly to the third, in which the spectator hears an answering chord in himself. Such emotional chords can not be superficial or without value; the feeling of such a picture can indeed deepen and purify the feeling of the spectator. The spirit at least is preserved from coarseness: such pictures tune it up, as a tuning fork does the strings of a musical instrument. But the subtilization and extension of this chord in time and space remained limited, and the potential power of art is not exhausted by it.

The word is an inner sound. It springs partly, perhaps principally, from the object denoted. But if the object is not seen, but only its name heard, the mind of the hearer receives an abstract impression only of the object dematerialized, and a corresponding vibration is immediately set up in the " heart." Thus a green, yellow, or red tree in a meadow are accidental realizations of the concept tree which we formed upon hearing the word.

The apt use of a word (in its poetical sense), its repetition, twice, three times, or even more frequently, according to the need of the poem, will not only tend to intensify the internal structure but also bring out unsuspected spiritual properties in the word itself. Further, frequent repetition of a word (a favorite game of children, forgotten in later life) deprives the word of its external reference. Similarly, the symbolic reference of a designated object tends to be forgotten and only the sound is retained. We hear this pure sound, unconsciously perhaps, in relation to the concrete or immaterial object. But in the latter pure sound exercises a direct impression on the soul. The soul attains to an objectless vibration, even more complicated, I might say more transcendent, than the reverberations released by the sound of a bell, a stringed instrument, or a fallen board. In this direction lie great possibilities for the literature of the future. This verbal potency has already been used in an embryonic form in *Serres Chaudes*. An ostensibly neutral word in its felt quality will become somber as Maeterlinck uses it. A familiar word like " hair," used in a certain way, intensifies an atmosphere of sorrow or despair. This is Maeterlinck's method. He makes us realize that thunder, lightning and a moon behind driving clouds are external, material means, which on the stage, even more than in nature, resemble the bogey-man of childhood: imaginings.

Inner forces do not lose their strength and effect so easily. [1] A word which has two meanings, the first direct, the second indirect, is the material of poetry and literature, which these arts alone can manipulate and through which they speak to the soul.

Something similar may be seen in the music of Wagner. His famous *Leitmotiv* is an attempt to give personality to his characters by something more than theatrical paraphernalia, make-up and light effects. His method of using a definite *Motiv* is a musical method. It creates a spiritual atmosphere by means of a musical phrase which precedes the hero, which he seems to radiate from any distance.

Musical sound acts directly on the soul and finds an echo there, since music is innate in man.
" Everyone knows that yellow, orange, and red suggest ideas of 'joy and plenty' " (Delacroix).
The above quotation shows the deep relations among the arts, and especially between music and painting. Goethe said that painting must consider this relation its ground, and by this prophetic remark he foretold the position of painting today. Painting stands, in fact, at the first stage of the road by which it will, according to its own possibilities, grow in the abstract sense and arrive finally at painterly *composition*.

FRANZ MARC: APHORISMS
Written at the front in early 1915.

1.

Every thing has its shell and kernel, semblance and being, mask and truth. The fact that we only grope at the shell, instead of seeing into the being of things, that we are so blinded by the mask of things, that we can not find the truth, —how does that refute the inner definiteness of the things?

25.

In the 20th century we shall live amongst strange faces, new pictures, and unheard-of sounds.
Many who are not filled with an inner passion will freeze and withdraw to the remnants of their memories. Woe to the demagogues who try to drag them out. Everything has its season, and the world has time.

31.

Traditions are a splendid thing; but they should be created, not lived on.

---

[1] Alas, this word, which in the past was used to describe the poetical aspirations of an artist's soul, has been misused and finally ridiculed. Was there ever a great word that the crowd did not try immediately to desecrate?

[1] A comparison of the work of Poe and Maeterlinck shows the course of artistic transition from the material to the abstract.

39.

The creative man honours the past by leaving it in peace and not by living on it. It was the tragedy of our fathers that they wanted, like the alchemists, to make gold out of venerable dust. In doing so they lost their " fortune." They ran the gamut of past cultures and lost the ability to create their own.

56.

Our old world of sensibility has slowly been eroded by the development of world knowledge; our poetic and graphic vision have been completely altered. What was at one time grasped as " subject matter " by our passion, is now analyzed by us into simple numerical relationships and vibrations. (This is also the reason for the understandable, but also rightly criticized poverty and emptiness of many modern, supposedly modern pictures.)
We no longer stop there. Our passion no longer sentimentally fights against the things, but looks for an escape, for its " taming through form " in the profound pictures that disclose the newly-comprehended natural laws before our astonished eyes.

67.

Humbly, almost hopelessly, the idea of an art of " pure form " developed some years ago. Its own justification hid behind apparent reasons and theories which did not provide the daring and purity of the new works with good company. Nobody had the courage to say simply that the justification lay in the new European outlook, in a new *Weltanschauung*, and that we were already living in the light of the new vision that—sooner or later—would reshape our art.
The path is strewn with misunderstandings. I shall only speak of one, which I have recognized as one of the worst: the habit of playing off, with a particularly cunning expression, the " How " in art against the " What." This argument presupposes that there could be no question at all of calling something art where the " How," the quality in art, is missing. It would at the most be a call for the dilettantes, since artists are only concerned with the " What," the content.

78.

Today we are replacing the use of natural law as an artistic means with the religious problem of the new content. The art of our epoch be doubtless closely analogous to the art of past, primitive times, though without the formalistic relationship which some archaists today are pointlessly striving for. It is equally certain that our age will be followed by another epoch of cooler maturity which, in turn, will again set up formal artistic laws (traditions) parallel to the contemporary happenings in the very far-off, mature, late-European age.

82.

I saw the picture that is reflected in the eyes of the moorhen when it dives: the thousand rings that enclose every small life, the blue of the whispering sky, absorbed by the lake, ecstatic reappearance in a different place—see, my friends, what pictures are: reappearance in a different place...

AUGUST MACKE: THE MASKS
From: *Der Blaue Reiter*. Editors: Kandisky/Franz Marc, Munich 1912, p. 21.

A sunny day, an overcast day, a Persian spear, a sacred vessel, a heathen idol, and a wreath of everlasting flowers, a Gothic church and a Chinese junk, the bows of a pirate ship, the word pirate, and the word holy, darkness, night, spring, cymbals and their sound and the shooting of battleships, the Egyptian sphinx and the patch on the cheek of a Parisian coquette.
The lamplight in Ibsen's and Maeterlinck's works, paintings of village streets and ruins, the mystery plays of the Middle Ages and the scaring of children, a landscape by van Gogh and a still life by Cézanne, the hum of propellers and the whinnying of horses, the battle cry in a cavalry charge and the war paint of the Indians, the cello and the bell, the shrill whistle of the locomotive and the cathedral-like atmosphere of a beech wood, the masks and stages of the Japanese and Greeks and the mysterious, muffled drumming of the Indian fakir.
Is not life more important than food, and the body more important than the clothing?
Incomprehensible ideas express themselves in comprehensible forms. Comprehensible as star, thunder, flower, as form, through our senses.
The form is our secret, because it is the expression of secret forces. Only through the form can we divine the secret powers, the " invisible God."
The senses are our bridge from the incomprehensible to the comprehensible. To look at plants and animals means to sense their secret. To hear thunder means to sense its secret. To understand the language of form means to be closer to the secret, to live. To create forms means to live. Are not children, who create directly from their mysterious sensibility, more creative than mere copiers of Greek form? Are not the natives artists, who have their own form, as strong as the phenomenon of thunder?
Thunder expresses itself, the flower, every force, expresses itself as form. And so does man. Something drives him as well, to find words for conceptions, clarity from obscurity, consciousness from unconsciousness. That is his life, his work.

PAUL KLEE: ON MODERN ART
Notes for a speech at the opening of an exhibition of modern art in Jena, 1924. Berne, 1945.

Let me use a metaphor, the metaphor of a tree. The artist has concerned himself with this variform world, and, let us assume, he has adjusted himself to a certain extent; quite quietly. He is well enough adjusted to bring some order into the fleeting manifestations and experiences of this world. I should like to compare this orientation concerning nature and life, this interwoven and ramified order, to the roots of a tree.
From these roots the sap rises to the artist, to pass through him and through his eyes.
Thus he takes the place of the trunk.
Pressed and moved by the power of the rising sap, he passes the things seen into his work.
Just as the crown of a tree spreads itself visibly to all sides in time and space, so does the work. Nobody would ever ask that the tree should form its crown exactly as its roots. Everyone will understand that there can be no exact mirror view between below and above. It is evident that the

different functions in various basic spheres will produce lively variations.

But people nevertheless try at times to forbid the artist, of all people, to vary from the original, although the composition alone demands that he should. He has even been accused of inability and intentional falsification.

And yet he does nothing but fulfill his function as trunk, and collects and passes on that which came from below. Neither serving nor governing, only mediating.

He thus occupies a truly modest position. And the beauty of the crown is not he himself, it has only passed through him. (p. 11).

Now to business, to the dimensions of the picture.

I have spoken of the relationship between crown and roots, between work and nature, and have explained the difference between the two spheres of earth and air, and between the different functions of the lower and the upper regions.

The work of art, which I compared to the crown of a tree, is the result of the necessity for distortion which comes from the contact with the specific dimensions of the pictorial. For that is the aim of the rebirth of nature.

What are then these specific dimensions?

To begin with, there are more or less limited formal things, such as line, intermediate tones, and colour.

The line is the most limited, being a matter of measurement alone. Its characteristics are longer or shorter lengths, obtuse or acute angles, radii, focal distances. Always measurable things! Measurement is the characteristic of this factor, and where the measurability is doubtful the line has not been used with absolute purity.

The tonalities, or, as they are also called, the intermediate tones, the many gradations between black and white, are of a somewhat different nature. This second factor is concerned with questions of weight. The one grade consists of denser or less dense white energy, another is more or less saturated with black. Each is gradated within itself. Apart from this, there are the black ones in relation to a white norm (on a white ground), the white ones in relation to a black norm (on the blackboard), or both together in relation to a medium grey norm.

Thirdly, there are the colours which apparently show quite different characteristics. For one can not evaluate them fully either by measurement or by weighing: where measurement and weighing can no longer find any difference between, for example, a pure yellow and a pure red area of the same size and the same degree of brightness, there is still one outstanding difference which we label with the words yellow and red.

In the same way one can compare salt and sugar, except for their saltiness and sweetness.

I would therefore like to call the colours qualities.

As we have seen, we have formal means of measurement, weight and quality, which, despite their fundamental differences, are nevertheless connected.

The way in which they are connected can be seen from the following short analysis.

Colour is primarily quality. Secondly it is weight, since it has not only a quality of colour, but also a quality of brightness. Thirdly it is also a measurable quality, for in addition to the values mentioned it has its boundaries, its size, its area, its measurability.

The intermediate tone is firstly weight, and secondly, in its expansion or limitation, it has a measurable quality.

The line, however, has only measurable qualities. (p. 17)

While the artist is doing his utmost to group the formal elements together as logically as possible, so that each one is given its essential place and does not encroach on the others, a lay spectator says devastatingly: it still doesn't look at all like uncle! The painter says to himself—if he has sufficient self-discipline—" to hell with uncle! I must get on with the essentials "... (p. 29)

I should now like to examine the dimensions of things in a new light, and try to show why the artist often arrives at an apparently arbitrary "deformation" of the natural object. It should be realized that he does not attach such primary importance to the natural appearance of the object as do the many realists who like to practice criticism.

He does not feel himself so strongly bound to these realities, because he does not see the essence of the natural creative process in these end-forms. To him the formative powers are much more important than the end-forms.

He is perhaps, without necessarily wanting to be, a philosopher. And if he does not declare this world, like an optimist, to be the best of all worlds, and also if he does not say that this world surrounding us is too bad to be taken as an exemplar, he would say yet:

This world that we can see is not the only one in existence! (p. 41)

Thus he looks at the things which nature presents him with, with penetrating eyes.

The deeper he looks, the easier it is for him to relate the contemporary views to the past, and the more the exclusive importance of creation as genesis impresses itself upon him in place of a finished picture of nature.

He then allows himself the thought that it is unlikely that creation is already complete, and, in doing so, extends that world-creative effort from backwards to forwards. Thus lending genesis permanency.

He goes still further.

He says to himself, remaining earthbound: this world has looked different in the past and will look different again in the future.

With regard to the non-terrestrial, however, he says: completely different forms may have developed on other planets. Such versatility in the natural ways of creation is a good training in form.

It can profoundly move the creator, and, versatile himself, he will nurture the freedom of development in his own creative work. Taking this into consideration, one can not blame him if he considers the contemporary stage of the visible world he happens to have been born into as accidentally retarded, retarded in time and place, all too retarded in comparison with his deeper vision and quicker emotions.

And is it not true that just the relatively small change of a view through a microscope presents the eye with pictures which we would all declare fantastic and eccentric if, without the intelligence to understand them, we saw them somewhere quite accidentally?

Mr. X, however, would clamour, enraged by such a picture in a sensational magazine: these are supposed to be natural forms? They are nothing but bad handicraft.

Is the artist then concerned with microscopy, history, palaeontology?

Only comparatively, only for the sake of versatility, not for the sake of keeping a scientific record of faithfulness to nature.

Only for the sake of freedom.

For the sake of a freedom which does not lead to specific

phases of development which at some stage occurred or will occur in nature, or which might be found replicated on other stars (this might some time be demonstrable).

For the sake of a freedom which only claims a right to the same versatility enjoyed by nature. From example to archetype!

MAX ERNST: WHAT IS SURREALISM?

From: Ausstellungskatalog Kunsthaus Zurich, 1934; reprinted in: *Max Ernst*, Gemaelde und Graphik 1920-1950, Bruehl 1951, p. 30.

"Le mot délit n'a, en général, pas été compris."
Paul Eluard

As the last superstition, as a sad remnant of the myth of creation, the fairy tale of the c r e a t i v e f u n c t i o n of the artist survived in occidental civilization. It was one of the first revolutionary acts of Surrealism to attack this myth and probably to destroy it forever with withering factual means, by emphatically insisting on the purely p a s s i v e role of the " author " in the mechanism of poetic inspiration; it exposed herewith all " active " control by reason, moral or aesthetic considerations as being contrary to inspiration. He may witness the creation of the work as a spectator, and follow its phases of development with disinterest or passion. As the poet listens to his automatic processes of thinking and notes them down, so does the painter project onto paper or canvas what his power of imagination inspires him with...

" The accidental encounter of a sewing machine and an umbrella on a dissecting table " (Lautréamont) is today a universally known, almost classic example for the phenomenon discovered by the Surrealists that t h e j u x t a p o s i t i o n o f t w o (o r m o r e) a p p a r e n t l y a l i e n e l e - m e n t s o n a n a l i e n p l a n e p r o m o t e s t h e m o s t p o t e n t p o e t i c c o m b u s t i o n. Countless individual and collective experiments (for example, those called the " *Cadavre exquis* ") have proved the utility of this process. It was discovered that the more a r b i t r a r y the juxtaposition of the elements, the more certain it was that a complete or partial transubstantiation of the things by the flying spark of poetry would take place. The joy in every successful metamorphosis does not originate from a miserable aesthetic urge for distraction. It rather stems from the ancient vital need of the intellect for emancipation from the chimerical and stultifying paradise of fixed memories, and from its urge to explore a new, incomparably larger sphere of experience, where the borders of the so-called inner world and the outer world (according to the classical philosophical concept) overlap more and more, and where they will probably one day (when preciser methods than the *écriture automatique* have been found) disappear completely...

If it is said then of the Surrealists that they are painters of an ever-changeable dream reality, it certainly does not mean that they copy their dreams (that would be descriptive, naive naturalism), or that each of them builds his own little world out of dream elements where he may deport himself in a friendly or malicious fashion (that would be " flight from time "); it means that they move freely, bravely, and matter-of-factly in the physically and psychically perfectly real (" surreal "), if still rather indefinite border region of the inner and outer worlds; that they classify what they see and experience there, and take action where their revolutionary

instincts prompt them.[1]) The fundamental difference between meditation and action (according to the classical philosophical concept) disappears with the fundamental differentiation between outer and inner world; hence the universal importance of Surrealism lies in the fact that after this discovery no sphere of life can remain closed to it. Thus plastic art as well, apparently alien to all automatism, had to join the Surrealist movement. In addition to the sculptures of Arp and Giacometti attention must be drawn to the surrealistic objects " à *fonctionnement symbolique* " (for example, Giacometti, " *Boule suspendue* "), and to the Utopian projects of whose poetic possibilities the reader will no doubt get an idea from the following description: " *De grandes automobiles, trois fois plus grandes que nature, seront reproduites (avec une minutie de détails surpassant celle des moulages les plus exacts) en plâtre ou en onyx, pour être enfermées, enveloppées de linge de femme, dans des sépultures, dont l'emplacement ne sera reconnaissables que par la présence d'une mince horloge de paille* " (Salvador Dali).

Already existing works of plastic art can function as poetic elements in Surrealistic experiments like any other " reality," as collective experiments aiming at irrationally beautifying Paris have shown: " *Les plus conventionelles des statues embelliraient merveilleusement les campagnes. Quelques femmes nues en marbre seraient du meilleur effet sur une grande plaine labourée. Des animaux dans les ruisseaux et des concils de graves personnages cravatés de noir dans les rivières formeraient de charmants écueils à la monotonie des flots. Le flanc des montagnes s'agrémenterait à ravir de toutes les pétrifications de la danse. Et pour faire la part de la mutilation indispensables, que de têtes sur le sol, que de mains sur les arbres, que de pieds sur le chaume!* " (Paul Eluard).

What is Surrealism? Anyone expecting a definition in answer to this question will have to remain disappointed until this movement has come to an end. My all too short remarks were intended to check to a certain degree the ever-increasing and to a certain extent already quite common confusion of ideas about the Surrealist movement. Otherwise I can do nothing better here than to refer the reader to A. Breton's " *Surrealistische Manifeste* " and " *Les vases communicants*." The fact that contradictions can be found in the successive attitudes of the Surrealists, and that such contradictions are continually recurring point to the fact that the movement is still in its prime. In overthrowing the relationships between the " realities " it could only help to accelerate the universal crisis of conscience and consciousness of our time.

OSKAR KOKOSCHKA: THE PROMETHEUS SAGA
(notes on my ceiling painting in London) [2]
From: OSKAR KOKOSCHKA, Schriften 1907-1955, Munich 1956, p. 413. First printed in *Das Werk*, volume 7/1952, p. 232.

I have been asked to make a few introductory remarks concerning my cycle of ceiling murals, " The Prometheus Saga " which I recently painted, and which is being shown in public for the first time at this year's Biennale. Despite the danger that this exposition will not measure up to contemporary usage—my excuse is that throughout my life I

---

[1]) In contradiction to Abstractivism, which intentionally limits its possibilities to the purely aesthetic reciprocal effects of colours, areas, volumes, lines, and space, etc., on one another. Apparently in order to help the old myth of creation onto its feet, as is shown by the collective name " *Abstraction, Création.*"

[2]) in Antoine Count Seilern's house in London.

82

have never painted according to the vogue—, I herewith confess that in this painting, my largest at least in area, I intentionally ignored all the internationally recognized taboos of the day. This painting was intended to exhibit objective content and space compatible with the European, who is conscious of his history. I used a concept of space into which I consciously inserted the fourth dimension of movement discovered in the Baroque period; this enables the spectator to follow to a certain extent chronologically the sequence of the events depicted from the beginning to the end. I know in advance that this admission must seem blasphemous to the Abstract painter, as ever since the dictatorship of the Fauves in Paris the reduction of the pictorial concept to two-dimensionality has been considered a matter of basic aesthetic principle. This may be legitimate where the problems of wall decoration are concerned. If, however, two-dimensionality is more a question of the *Weltanschauung* of bearded, long-haired youths who can be found today in conventions in every metropolis in the world discussing the existential problem of the new society, and who, like sansculottes, would like to shed their clothes along with European tradition in preparation for the world revolution which is to surpass even Rousseau's " Back to Nature," then, at my age, I resign and am patient. So far, each new generation has proved that every new must will eventually mature into wine. Even the widely dreaded danger in the political field that man will become impersonal and turn into an isotype of bureaucratic statistics, is no doubt exaggerated. With premeditation and foreknowledge I have reached back into the past for the intellectual means of expression used before European society decided to ignore its own culture. I believe that I, without being guilty of intellectual plagiarism or plundering, preserve the European artistic tradition. It is my opinion that not every generation must begin from the beginning, and that the artist should leave theorizing to the dogmatists. Looking at it from the social point of view, I have come to the conclusion, as an active participant in the first World War and as a passive one in the second, that the creative artist's task is the forming of his visual experience and thus of existence...

A proletarianized society of today needs, above all, a link with the past, so that not every individual in his intellectual arrogance considers himself called upon to undertake the work of destruction, imagining that the certain awkward, loose tile will only hit his neighbour's head. If an alert social conscience does not do so, then at least his reasoning should warn the creative artist that an artistic language which is not communicable becomes pointless if it does not convey the experience which is constantly renewing our humanity as a message from the I to the you. It is, in fact, experience which transforms us from a herd into individuals. To live in an ivory tower is just as pointless for an aesthete. That is just as useless and unsocial as a life in an air raid shelter or under the earth. We should not forget that after all the world is not made for one person alone, and does not go round just for us.

... The more we cling to Utopias today and try to bypass existence, the present, the more we invite the faulty results of a focus which ignores the closeness of reality. In the same proportion that our existence more and more lacks the interpretation of a final secret, despite all analytical materialism, the further the dispute over the forming of visual experience is removed from the sphere of limited aesthetics. The creative power has a share in being; the picture, in becoming a symbol, stops being nothing but a rationalistic emblem. For that reason my Prometheus picture should not be considered as an individual achievement, for humanity anonymously contributed towards it, the same humanity which today, East and West together, is starting its journey to the moon propelled by its own petard.

MAX BECKMANN: MY THEORY OF PAINTING
Lecture held on July 21st, 1938, in the New Burlington Gallery, London.
From: Benno Reifenberg and Wilhelm Hausenstein, *Max Beckmann*, Munich 1949, p. 47.

I am very sorry that I can not speak to you in English. Perhaps I shall be able to do so on some later occasion. Before I begin to give you an explanation, an explanation which is practically impossible, I would like to emphasize that I have never been politically active in any way. I have only tried to present my view of the world as plainly as possible.

Painting is a difficult business. It demands the whole of a person, body and soul—and so I have blindly passed by many things that belong to the real and political life. I take it, however, that there are two worlds: the spiritual world, and the world of political reality. Both are manifestations of life, but though they sometimes overlap, they are basically very different. I must leave it to you to decide which of the two is more important.

What I try to show in my work is the idea which hides behind so-called reality. I strive to find the bridge that leads from the visible to the invisible, like the famous cabalist who once said: " If one wishes to understand the invisible, one must penetrate as far as possible into the visible."

My constant aim is to capture the magic of the so-called reality, and translate this reality into painting—to make the invisible visible through reality. It sounds perhaps paradoxical, but it is actually reality that forms the secret of our existence.

What helps me most in this task is the penetration of space. Height, breadth, and depth are the three phenomena which I have to transfer onto one plane in order to form the abstract surface of the picture; in this way I protect myself from the infinity of space. My figures come and go, as luck or misfortune bids them. I try to transfix them, stripped of their accidental superficial characteristics.

One of my problems is to find the I, which has only one shape and is immortal—to find it in animals and people, in the heaven and hell which together form the world in which we live.

Space and space again is the infinite deity that surrounds us and in which we ourselves are contained.

That then is what I try to express through my painting, a function different from poetry and music, but for me a fateful necessity.

When spiritual, metaphysical, important or unimportant events take place in my life, I can only retain them through my painting. It is not the theme that is important, but the transposition of the theme into the abstraction of the plane through painting. For this reason I hardly need abstract forms, for every object is already unreal enough; so unreal that I can only make it real through painting.

Often, very often, I am alone. My studio in Amsterdam, a huge old tobacco storage room, is populated again in my memory with figures from the old and new times, moved like an ocean by storm and sun, and always present in my thoughts.

Then the forms take shape and seem palpable to me in the great emptiness and uncertainty of the space that I call God.

Sometimes the constructive rhythm of the cabala helps me when my thoughts about Oanes Dagon wander to the last days of the sunken continents. The streets, with their men, women, and children, with their great ladies and whores, their maids and duchesses, are made of the same stuff. It seems to me then that I meet them like ambiguous dreams, in Samothrace and Piccadilly, and in Wall Street. They are Eros and the longing for oblivion.

All these things appear to me in black and white, like virtue and crime. Yes, black and white are my two elements. It is my luck or my misfortune that I can not see everything in black or everything in white. It would be so much simpler and clearer if I could, but reality does not permit it. Many dream of seeing only the white and really beautiful, o r the black, ugly and destructive. But I have to accept both, for only in both, only in black a n d white, I am able to recognize God in his oneness, as he always and again works on the ever-changing drama of everything mortal.

I have unintentionally gone from fundamentals to form, to transcendental ideas. A sphere which is by no means mine, but nevertheless I am not ashamed of.

In my opinion all the important things in art since Ur of the Chaldees, since Tel Halaf and Crete, have sprung from a profound feeling for the mystery of our existence. All objective spirits strive for self-representation. I try to capture this I in my life and in my art.

Art is creative for the sake of representation, not for entertainment—for the sake of transformation, not as a game. It is the search for our I which drives us along the infinite and never-ending path that we all must travel. My means of expressing my I is painting; there are, of course, other ways of reaching this goal—literature, philosophy or music, for example, but as a painter, blessed or damned to a terrible sensuous intensity, I must seek my wisdom with my eyes. I repeat, with my eyes, for nothing would be more laughable or meaningless than a " philosophical concept " painted purely intellectually, without the terrible rage of the senses, which grabs at every visible form of beauty or ugliness. If, out of the figures which I have found within the visible, literary themes emerge—such as portraits, landscapes, or recognizable compositions—they have all nevertheless sprung from the senses, in this case from the eyes, and every intellectually conceived theme is also translated into form, colour, and space.

All spiritual and transcendental elements are fused in painting by the uninterrupted activity of the eyes. Every shade of colour in a flower, face, tree, fruit, lake, or a mountain, is diligently absorbed by the power of the senses, which is assisted, in a manner unknown to us, by the work of the intellect. And finally the strength and weakness of the soul, the true and never-changing centre of power that enables the intellect and senses to give expression to the personality. It is the strength of the soul that forces the intellect to practice continually and to broaden its concept of space.

Something of this has perhaps been captured in my pictures.

ERNST WILHELM NAY: ON " CHROMATIC COUNTERPOINT "

From: ERNST WILHELM NAY, *Vom Gestaltwert der Farbe*, Munich 1955, p. 21.

If I take the difference between cold and warm colours as the basic theme of colours, and select the group of warm colours as the dominant, then I can play off three values of the warm group of colours, perhaps orange, cinnabar, madder pink, against two values of the cold colours, perhaps Paris blue light with cobalt blue light. I have the proportion 3 : 2. These colours, used without any variation from the original, demand that their interrelationship be made visible. A colour that is related to both groups now must be found. Grey is unrelated. The related colour is violet, containing red and blue, an intensification of grey. If I now wish to show that these three colour groups sound warm, cold, and violet in between, I add, in order to agitate them, a colour completely alien to the tutti sound, a colour which has nothing to do with this counterpoint, but which, in so far as I insert it in small values, now makes the process as such completely visible—a permanent green. In small values it causes the necessary disturbance and emphasizes the actual effective tensions. Thus the permanent green has a contrapuntal effect.

Fritz Winter Vignette for the Exhibition Catalogue of the Kestner Society, 1951

BIOGRAPHIES AND LITERATURE
ON THE ARTISTS IN THIS BOOK

WILLI BAUMEISTER

Born January 22, 1889 in Stuttgart; died there August 31, 1955.

Began as a house-painter. Studied from 1906 on with Hoelzel at the Stuttgart Academy of Fine Arts, friendship with Schlemmer and Meyer-Amden. 1914-1918 military service. 1919-1922 period of "wall-pictures." 1923 Paris, contact with Ozenfant, Le Corbusier, and Fernand Léger. Machine and sports pictures. 1928-1933 Professor at the Frankfort School of Art, pictures with sand application. Dismissed from his post in 1933. Since 1936 completely non-objective pictures. 1939-1944 employed at Herbert's Institute of Painting Technique in Wuppertal. 1946 teacher at the Stuttgart Academy of Fine Arts.

OWN WRITINGS: *Das Unbekannte in der Kunst*, Stuttgart 1947.—"Warum ich gegenstandslos male," in *Die Kunst*, 48 (1950), p. 325.

BIBLIOGRAPHY: Werner Graeff. *W. B.*, including articles by Waldemar Georges, Christian Zervos, H. Hildebrandt, and K. K. Duessel, Stuttgart 1927.—Will Grohmann. *W. B.*, Paris 1931.—Will Grohmann. "*W. B.*," in *Chronique de la vie artistique*, XI, Antwerp 1931.—Eduardo Westerdahl. "*W. B.* Canarias 1934*," in *Cahiers d'Art*, 20/21 (1945-1946), p. 342. —Egon Vietta. "Der spaete B.," in *Die Kunst* I (1948), p. p. 97.—Will Grohmann. *W. B.*, Stuttgart 1952 (with extensive bibliography).—Franz Roh. "Persoenliche Erinnerungen an W. B.," in *Die Kunst* 54 (1956), p. 210.

MAX BECKMANN

Born February 12, 1884 in Leipzig; died December 27, 1950 in Brooklyn, N. Y.

1899-1903 studied with Frithjof Smith at the Weimar Academy. 1906 Villa Romana Prize, travelled to Florence and Paris. 1909-1914 Berlin, member of the Berlin Secession, which he left in 1911. 1914-1915 medical orderly in the army. 1915-1933 Frankfort on the Main. 1925 Professor at the Frankfort School of Art until his dismissal, 1933, by the National Socialists. 1929-1932 various stays in Paris. 1933-1937 Berlin. 1937 emigration to Paris. 1938-1947 Amsterdam, Holland. 1947-1949 Professor at the School of Fine Arts, Washington University, St. Louis, Miss. 1949 teacher at the Brooklyn Museum School of Art, Brooklyn, N. Y.

OWN WRITINGS: "Gedanken ueber zeitgemaesse und unzeitgemaesse Kunst," in *Pan.* II (1912), No. 17; *cf.* Franz Marc. "Anti-Beckmann," in *Pan* II (1912), No. 19.—"Aeusserungen" zu "Das neue Programm," in *Kunst und Kuenstler*, 1914, p. 301.—*Briefe im Kriege*. Berlin 1916; new edition, Munich 1955.—*Vorwort zum Katalog der Ausstellung in Mannheim*, 1928.—"Drei Briefe an eine Malerin," und "Meine Theorie der Malerei," printed in Reifenberg and Hausenstein. *M. B.*, Munich 1949.—*Tagebuecher 1940-1950*, compiled by Mathilde Q. Beckmann, edited by Erhard Goepel, Munich 1955.

BIBLIOGRAPHY: Karl Scheffler. "M. B.," in *Kunst und Kuenstler* Xi (1913), p. 297.—Hans Kaiser. *Die Kunst M. B.'s*,

Max Beckmann Woman with Candle
Woodcut, 1920

Berlin 1913.—Benno Reifenberg, *Ganymed* III (1921), p. 37.—
—Curt Glaser, Julius Meier-Graefe, Wilhelm Fraenger, and Wilhelm Hausenstein, *M. B.*, Munich 1924.—Georg Swarzenski. *Das Neue Frankfurt*, No. 4 (1927).—Heinrich Simon. *M. B.*, Leipzig 1930.—Wolfgang Schoene. *M. B.*, Berlin 1947. —Fritz Nemitz. "M. B.," in *Die Kunst* I (1948), p. 68.—
—Benno Reifenberg and Wilhelm Hausenstein. *M. B.*,, Munich 1949.—Franz Roh. "Zum Tode M. B.'s," in *Kunstchronik* 4 (1951), No. 2, p. 25.—*In Memoriam M. B.*, first publication of

the M. B. Society, Frankfort on the Main 1953.—Erhard Goepel. *M. B. der Zeichner*, Munich 1954.—Erhard Goepel. *M. B. in seinen spaeten Jahren*, Munich 1955.—Hans Maria Wingler. *M. B., Holzschnitte, Radierungen und Lithographien*, Feldafing 1955.

LOVIS CORINTH

Born July 21, 1858 at Tapiau, East Prussia; died July 17, 1925 at Zandvoort, Holland.

1876-1880 at the Koenigsberg Academy of Painting. 1880 in Munich, studied with Defregger and Ludwig Loefftz. 1884 to Paris via Antwerp. 1887-1891 Koenigsberg. 1891-1902 Munich. 1902 moved to Berlin. Leading member of the Secession. From 1918 on several long stays in his country house on Walchensee, Upper Bavaria.

OWN WRITINGS: *Das Erlernen der Malerei*, Berlin 1908.— —*Legenden aus dem Kuenstlerleben*, Berlin 1908.—*Gesammelte Schriften*, Berlin 1920.—*Selbstbiographie*, Leipzig 1926.

BIBLIOGRAPHY: Rudolf Klein. *L. C.*, Berlin 1908.— —Georg Biermann. *L. C.*, Bielefeld and Leipzig 1913.—Karl Schwarz. *Das graphische Werk L. C.'s*, Berlin 1917.—Lovis Corinth and Wilhelm Hausenstein. *Von und ueber Corinth*, Leipzig 1921.—*Ausstellungskatalog Hans Goltz*, Munich 1924 (with a list of the books illustrated by him and portfolios of graphic art).—Georg Biermann. *Der Zeichner L. C.*, Dresden

Lovis Corinth Self-Portrait
Drawing, 1913

1924.—*Ausstellungskatalog der Kunsthalle Bern, 1924.—Ausstellungskatalog der Galerie Wiltschek* (with an introduction by Curt Glaser), Berlin 1925.—Alfred Kuhn. *L. C.*, Berlin 1925. —Paula Steiner. *L. C., dem Ostpreussen* (with a contribution by L. C.), Koenigsberg 1925.—*Ausstellungskatalog der National-galerie*, Berlin 1926.—*Ausstellungskatalog der Akademie der Kuenste (Das Graphische Werk)*, Berlin 1926.—*Ausstellung der Berliner Sezession*, Berlin 1928.—Charlotte Behrend-Corinth. "Vom Leben und Schaffen Corinths," in *Das Kunstblatt* XV (1931), p. 198.—*Ausstellungskatalog der Kunsthalle Basel*, 1936. —Alfred Rohde. *Der junge Corinth*, Berlin 1941.—Charlotte Behrend-Corinth. *Mein Leben mit L. C.*, Hamburg 1947.— —*Ausstellungskatalog des Landesmuseums Hannover*, 1950.—Gert von der Osten. *L. C.*, Hanover and Munich 1955.

OTTO DIX

Born December 2, 1891 at Untermhaus near Gera; lives in Duesseldorf and Hemmenhofen on Lake Constance.

Comes from a working-class family. 1905-1909 apprenticeship as house-painter in Gera. 1910-1914 studied at the Dresden School of Arts and Crafts. 1914-1918 soldier on the western front. 1917 publication of his war cycle (50 etchings), which made him famous. After the war four years study at the Dresden Academy. 1922-1925 free-lance artist in Duesseldorf, 1925-1933 Professor at the Dresden Academy, then removed from his position and branded as "decadent." 1936 moved to Hemmenhofen on Lake Constance, work on religious topics. 1939 arrested by the Gestapo. 1945, as conscript in the German Home Guard, spent a short time as prisoner of war in France. Has taken over a painting class at the Duesseldorf Academy, 1950.

BIBLIOGRAPHY: P. F. Schmidt. *O. D.*, Cologne 1923.— —W. Wolfradt, "O. D.," in *Junge Kunst* (Vol. 41), Leipzig 1925.—Franz Roh. *Nach-Expressionismus*, Leipzig 1925.—*Austel-lungskatalog* (with a preface by Walter Passarge), Mannheim 1951.

Otto Dix Nocturnal Scene
Woodcut, 1920

MAX ERNST

Born April 2, 1891 at Bruehl near Cologne; lives at Sedona, Arizona.

Studied philosophy and history of art at Bonn University. Selftaught painter. 1913 participation in the First German Autumn Salon, Berlin. 1914-1918 military service. 1917 participation in the "Dada Gallery" exhibition in Zurich. 1919 founded the group "Dada W/3" in Cologne, together with Arp and Baargeld. 1920 exhibition of his "collages" in Paris. 1922 moved to Paris, friendship with Breton, Eluard, Picabia, Man Ray; founded the Surrealist group in Paris. 1925 participated in the first exhibition of the Surrealists in Paris. 1926 *Frottages*. 1929 *La Femme 100 Têtes*. 1934 *Une Semaine de Bonté*. 1939-1940 interned in the south of France. 1941-1945 New York. Since 1946 living, though not permanently, in Arizona and Huismes, France.

OWN WRITINGS: *Beyond Painting*, The Documents of Modern Art, ed. Robert Motherwell, New York 1948 (with extensive bibliography).

BIBLIOGRAPHY: L. Aragon. *La peinture au défi*, Paris 1930. —*Cahiers d'Art*," M. E., Oeuvres de 1919 à 1936," Paris 1937. —André Breton. *Le Surréalisme et la peinture*, Paris 1945.—J. Bosquet and M. Tapié. *M. E.*, Paris 1950.—*Ausstellungskatalog M. E.*, edited by Lothar Pretzell, Bruehl 1951 (the best German compilation of the last few years).—*Cahiers d'Art* 28 (1953), p. 93.

LYONEL FEININGER

Born July 17, 1871 in New York, N. Y.; died there January 31, 1956.

Both parents, of German extraction, were musicians. F. himself used to play and compose. Went to Hamburg, 1887, in order to study music, but entered the School of Arts and

Lyonel Feininger Cathedral
From the first *Bauhaus* Proclamation, 1917

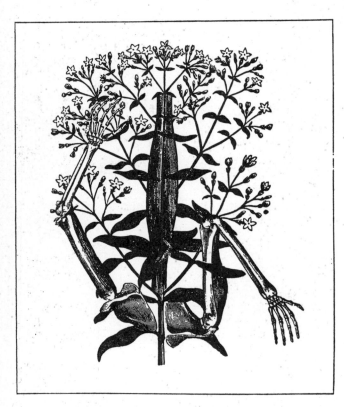

Max Ernst "First Visible Poem No. 1"
Drawing, 1934

Crafts there instead. Afterwards Berlin Academy. 1892-1893 Académie Colarossi, Paris. 1893-1906 Berlin, artist for the *Ulk* and *Lustige Blaetter*. 1906-1907 in Paris as contributor to the *Chicago Sunday Tribune*. 1908 back in Berlin, and awakening interest in painting . 1911 trip to Paris, met Delaunay and the Cubists. 1913 invited by the *Blaue Reiter* to exhibit at the First German Autumn Salon. 1919-1933 teacher at the *Bauhaus*, first in Weimar, then in Dessau. 1924 cofounder of the group *Die Blauen Vier*, the other members being Kandinsky, Klee, and Jawlensky. 1936 return to the U.S.A., where he taught art at Mills College, California.

BIBLIOGRAPHY: W. Wolfradt. *L. F.*, Leipzig 1924.—A. J. Schardt and A. H. Barr. *L. F.*, Museum of Modern Art, New York 1944 (with extensive bibliography).—*Ausstellungskatalog der Kestner-Gesellschaft*, Hanover 1954 (with some excerpts from letters).

WERNER GILLES

Born August 29, 1894 at Rheydt, Rhineland; lives as much as possible on Ischia, Italy, otherwise in Munich.

Werner Gilles "Orfeo" Lithograph, 1947
State Collection of Graphic Art, Munich

After studying at the Cassel and Weimar Academies, teacher at the *Bauhaus* with Feininger, 1919. 1921-1924 Italy, sometimes working in painted glass and as a copyist to earn his living. 1925 mainly in Duesseldorf. 1927-1928 France. 1930 Rome Prize. 1933-1936 Berlin and Baltic Sea. 1936-1941 Italy. 1946-1948 Schwarzenbach on the Saale.

BIBLIOGRAPHY: Otto Galley. "W. G.," in *Das Kunstblatt* XIV (1930), p. 277.—Horst Georges. "W. G.," in *Das Kunstblatt* I (1949), p. 5.—Werner Haftmann. *Deutsche Maler*, Steinheim a. M. (1949).—*Ausstellungskatalog der Kestner-Gesellschaft*, Hanover 1949.—Kurt Kusenberg. *Bilder aus Ischia*, Baden-Baden 1953.—Hans Konrad Roethel. "W. G.," in *Die Kunst* 53 (1954), p. 17.

Karl Hofer Lithograph
State Collection of Graphic Art, Munich

ERICH HECKEL

Born July 31, 1883 at Doebeln, Saxony; lives at Hemmenhofen on Lake Constance.

1901 met Schmidt-Rottluff; they studied architecture together with Fritz Schumacher at the Dresden Technological Institute. About 1905, founding of the Artists' Community *Bruecke*, together with Kirchner. Resigned from his job at the architectural studio of Wilhelm Kreis in 1906, and definitely turned to painting. 1911 moved to Berlin. 1914 volunteer medical orderly in Flanders. 1918-1941 permanent residence in Berlin and travelling. 1937 branded by the National Socialists as "decadent." 1941-1943 Carinthia. During air raids on Berlin, 1944, lost his home and studio together with many works, and all his xylographic presses, etching plates and lithograph stones. Since 1944 at Hemmenhofen on Lake Constance. 1949-1956 Professor at the Karlsruhe Academy.

Erich Heckel Self-Portrait Woodcut, 1917
State Collection of Graphic Art, Munich

OWN WRITINGS: "Brief ueber Munch und die *Bruecke*," in *Die Schanze* I (1951), p. 6.

BIBLIOGRAPHY: Paul Westheim. "E. H.," in *Das Kunstblatt* I (1917), p. 161.—Karl Scheffler. "E. H.," in *Kunst und Kuenstler* XVI (1918), p. 249.—Gustav Schiefler. "E. H.'s graphisches Werk," in *Das Kunstblatt* II (1918), p. 288.—Max Sauerlandt. "E. H., Aquarelle," in *Genius* III (1921), p. 73. —Eckart von Sydow. "E. H. als Graphiker," in *Der Cicerone* XIII (1921), p. 1.—Ernst Gosebruch. "E. H., Triptychon aus dem Jahre 1913," in *Museum der Gegenwart* I (1930). p. 30.— —Max Sauerlandt. "E. H.'s Bilder von der Flensburger Foerde," in *Schleswig-Holsteinisches Jahrbuch* XIX (1930), p. IX.—Ludwig Thormaehlen. *E. H.*, Leipzig 1931.—Erik Geller.

"Neuere Landschaften des Malers E. H.," in *Die Tat*, Jena 1935.—H. Koehn. *E. H.*, Berlin 1948.—Paul Ortwin Rave. *E. H.*, Berlin 1948.—Ernst Gosebruch. *E. H., Werke aus vier Jahrzehnten*, Cologne 1948.—Ludwig Thormaehlen. *E. H.*, Karlsruhe 1953.

KARL HOFER

Born October 11, 1878 at Karlsruhe; died April 3, 1955 in Berlin.

Studied at the Karlsruhe Academy with Thoma and L. von Kalckreuth; with the latter to Stuttgart in 1902. 1900 first stay in Paris. 1903-1908, helped by the Swiss collector Dr. Th. Reinhart, he lived in Rome. 1908-1913 Paris. 1913 Berlin. 1914-1917 interned in France. 1919 Professor at the Berlin Academy. 1925 first landscapes from Ticino. 1930-1931 abstract experiments. Dismissed from his position as academy professor in 1933. Lost a great number of his works in an air raid, March 1943; painted some of the lost pictures again. 1945 Professor at the Berlin Academy of Fine Arts, became 1947 its president.

OWN WRITINGS: *Vorwort* to his *Ausstellung bei Flechtheim*, Berlin 1931.—"Wege der Kunst," in *Bildende Kunst* I (1947), Nos. 3-5.—"Das Selbstverständliche und das Artistische in der Kunst," in *Thema* 1949, No. 1.—*Aus Leben und Kunst* (autobiography), Berlin 1952.—*Rede zur Eroeffnung der zweiten Ausstellung des deutschen Kuenstlerbundes*, Cologne 1952, pamphlet, not for sale.

BIBLIOGRAPHY: Benno Reifenberg. *K. H.*, Leipzig 1924. —*Ausstellung der Kunsthalle Mannheim* (his complete work), Mannheim 1928.—*Kollektiv-Ausstellung K. H., 55. Ausstellung der Berliner Sezession*, Berlin 1928.—Adolf Jannasch. *K. H.*, Potsdam 1946.—*Festgabe an Karl Hofer zum 70. Geburtstag*, edited by Gerhard Strauss, Potsdam (1949).

ALEXEJ VON JAWLENSKY

Born March 13, 1864 in Kuslowo, Province of Twer, Russia; died March 15, 1941 at Wiesbaden.

After training at the military academy, as lieutenant to Moscow, 1884, transferred to St. Petersburg, 1889; there he studied at the Academy under Rjepin. Left the army as captain, 1896, and went to Munich with Marianna von Werefkin. Studied at the Azbé School. Met Kandinsky and Father Willibrod Verkade. 1909 member of the New Artists' Association. Went to Switzerland, 1914, where he painted his *Variations on a Landscape Theme*. 1917 Zurich. 1921 Wiesbaden. Joined the group of the *Blaue Vier*, 1924. From 1929 on, progressive arthritis. 1934-1938 painted the small abstract heads (*Meditations*).

BIBLIOGRAPHY: Mila Escherich. *A. v. J.*, Wiesbaden 1934. —*Ausstellung bei Egon Guenther*, Mannheim 1947 (with an introduction by Wilhelm Monfang).—*Ausstellung bei Hanna Bekker vom Rath*, Frankfort 1954 (with an introduction by Hans Luehdorf).—Clemens Weiler. *A. v. J., der Maler und Mensch*, Wiesbaden 1955.

WASSILY KANDINSKY

Born December 5, 1866 in Moscow, Russia; died December 13, 1944 in Paris.

Studied law and economics in Moscow. Lecturer at Dorpat University. 1897 studied art with Azbé in Munich, later

Alexej von Jawlensky Self-Portrait
Pencil Drawing, 1912

Wassily Kandinsky
Woodcut, 1924

with Stuck at the Academy. 1901 President of the Artists' Association "Phalanx," and until 1903 teacher at their private art school. 1904-1908 travels with Gabriele Muenter. 1906 back in Munich, 1909 founding of the "New Artists' Association"; 1911 resignation, together with Muenter and Marc. Exhibition of the *Blaue Reiter* and publication of the almanac the following year. 1914 Switzerland; 1916 to Moscow via Stockholm. 1918 member of the art committee at the People's Commissariat and teacher at the State Workshops for Arts and Crafts in Moscow. 1919 director of the State Museum for Painting. By 1921 he had established, respectively enlarged more than 30 provincial museums. 1920 teacher of theory of art at Moscow University. Back in Germany since the end of 1921. 1922 *Bauhaus*, Weimar, later Dessau. After the closing of the *Bauhaus* through the National Socialists in 1933, to Paris; participated in the activities of the group "*Abstraction – Création*." 1939 became naturalized in France.

OWN WRITINGS: *Ueber das Geistige in der Kunst* (written in 1910), Munich 1912.—*Der Blaue Reiter*, edited by W. K. and Franz Marc, Munich 1912.—*Klaenge*, Munich (1913).——*Rueckblicke*, Berlin 1913.—*Punkt und Linie zur Flaeche*, Bauhausbuecher IX, 1926.—*Franz Marc*, Paris 1936.—List of publications and reprints of the most important ones in *Essays ueber Kunst und Kuenstler*, edited and with a commentary by Max Bill, Stuttgart 1955.

BIBLIOGRAPHY: H. Zehder. *W. K.*, Dresden 1920.—Will Grohmann. *W. K.*, Leipzig 1925.—Will Grohmann. "*K.*,"

Alexander Kanoldt "Olevano" Lithograph, 1924
State Collection of Graphic Art, Munich

in *Cahiers d'Art*, Paris 1931.—Vordemberge-Gildewart. *K.*, Amsterdam 1944.—Hilla Rebay. "In Memory of W.K., A Survey of the Artist's Paintings and Writings, New York 1945," in *Cahiers d'Art* 20/21 (1945-1946).—Marcel Arland. *K.*, Paris 1947.—Max Bill. *Album K.*, Basel 1949.—Charles Estienne. *K.*, Paris 1950.—Carola Giedion-Welcker. "*K.*'s Malerei als Ausdruck eines geistigen Universalismus," in *Das Werk* No. 4, 1950.—Max Bill. *K.*, Paris 1951.

ALEXANDER KANOLDT

Born September 29, 1881 at Karlsruhe; died January 24, 1939 in Berlin.

Son of the painter Edmund Kanoldt. 1889-1901 at the Karlsruhe School of Arts and Crafts, 1901-1904 at the Academy. 1906 awakening of his personal style after seeing works by Cézanne, Seurat (*La Grande Jatte*) and Signac at an exhibition at Karlsruhe. 1908 free-lance artist in Munich. 1909 charter member and secretary of the New Artists' Association. After its dissolution 1913, charter member of the Munich New Secession, 1920 resignation because of its lack of program. Friendship with Erbsloeh; about 1925 worked with Karl Mense and Georg Schrimpf, the exponents of the New Objectivity in Munich. 1925 Professor at the Breslau Academy. 1932 appointed to the Berlin Academy.

BIBLIOGRAPHY: J. A. Beringer. *Badische Malerei 1770-1920*, Karlsruhe (2nd edition) 1922.—Richard Hamann. "A. K.," in *Deutsche Kunst und Dekoration* LIII (1923-1924), p. 117 et seq.—Alfred Mayer. "A. K.," in *Deutsche Kunst und Dekoration* LVI (1925), p. 153 et seq.—Franz Roh. *Nach-Expressionismus*, Leipzig 1925.

Wassily Kandinsky
From the Cover of the *Blaue Reiter*
Woodcut, 1912

ERNST LUDWIG KIRCHNER

Born May 6, 1880 at Aschaffenburg; died June 15, 1938 at Frauenkirch near Davos, Switzerland.

1901-1902 studied architecture with Fritz Schumacher in Dresden. Two terms at the W. Debschitz and Hermann Obrist School of Art in Munich. 1904 return to Dresden. Founded, 1905, together with Heckel and Schmidt-Rottluff, the "Artists' Community *Bruecke*." 1911 moved to Berlin. During the summer months often on Fehmarn island. 1913 dissolution of the *Bruecke*. Joined, 1914, the army as volunteer. 1916 nervous breakdown, for some time in a sanatorium in the Taunus. 1917 Davos. Settled at Frauenkirch in 1918. Took his own life because of his defamation in Germany.

OWN WRITINGS: *Chronik der Bruecke* (not published), partly reprinted in the exhibition catalogue of the *Bruecke*, Bern 1948.—"Glaubensbekenntnisse eines Malers," in *Die Literatur-Gesellschaft* V (1919), reprinted in *Kunstblatt* 1919, p. 168.—A number of essays about himself under the pen-name Louis de Marsalle in various periodicals, among others in *Genius*. Four posthumous essays in *Galerie und Sammler*, No. 4, Zurich 1939, p. 70.—"Aus nachgelassenen Briefen," in *Das Kunstwerk* III (1951).

BIBLIOGRAPHY: Max Lehrs, "E. L. K.," in *Die Graphischen Kuenste* (1911), p. 49.—L. Burchard. "E. L. K.," in *Belvedere* (1913), p. 146.—P. F. Schmidt. *Kunstchronik* N. F. XXX (1918-1919), p. 481.—Karl Scheffler, *Kunst und Kuenstler* XVIII (1919), p. 217.—Gustav Schiefler, *Die Graphik E. L.*

E. L. *Kirchner* Woodcut, 1913
State Collection of Graphic Art, Munich

K.'s, Volume I, Berlin 1920; Volume II, Berlin 1926.—Will Grohmann. K., *Zeichnungen*, Dresden 1925.—Will Grohmann. *Das Werk E. L. K.'s*, Munich 1926.—Rosa Schapire. "E, L. K.," in *Der Kreis*, Hamburg 1927, p. 143.—Walter Kern. "E. L. K., seine Bilder von 1907-1929," in *Das Kunstblatt* XIV (1930), p. 160.—*Ausstellungskatalog der Bruecke*, Bern 1948.—W. Schmalenbach. "E. L. K.," in *Das Werk* 1948, No. 1.—Bernard S. Myers. "E. L. K. and *Die Bruecke*," in *Magazine of Art* XLV, New York 1952, p. 20.—Hans Maria Wingler. *E. L. K.*, Feldafing 1954.—*Ausstellungskatalog E. L. K.*, Wuerttembergischer Kunstverein, Stuttgart 1956.

E. L. *Kirchner* Mountain Melancholy (Self-Portrait)
Woodcut, 1926. State Collection of Graphic Art, Munich

PAUL KLEE

Born January 18, 1879 at Muenchenbuchsee near Bern, Switzerland; died June 29, 1940 at Muralto near Locarno.

His father was a musician from Bavaria, his mother a native of Basel. He played in the Bern orchestra already when still a boy. But then turned to painting. 1898 attended the L. Knirr School of Painting in Munich; 1900 pupil of Stuck. 1901 journey to Italy. 1902-1906 Bern. 1903-1905 drawings and etchings, partly influenced by Hodler. 1916 moved to Munich, artistic relationship to Kubin. 1911, met the members of the New Artists' Association. 1912 journey to Paris, meeting with Delaunay, whose essay on light he translated. 1911 participation in the exhibition of the *Blaue Reiter*. 1914 charter member of the New Munich Secession. April 1914 journey to Tunisia with Macke and Moilliet. 1916-1918 non-combatant soldier. 1920 one-man show at H. Goltz, Munich.

E. L. *Kirchner* Dancers
Woodcut, 1935

1921 appointed to the *Bauhaus* by Gropius. 1924 member of the group *Die Blauen Vier*. 1925 participation in the first exhibition of the Surrealists in Paris. 1929 journey to Egypt. 1930 appointed to the Duesseldorf Academy by Kaesbach. Dismissed in 1933; moved to Bern.

OWN WRITINGS: Excerpts from the *Tagebuecher* in the monographs by Zahn (1920) and Hausenstein (1921).—" Schoepferische Konfession," in *Tribuene der Kunst und Zeit*, Volume XIII, 1920.—*Wege des Naturstudiums*, Staatliches *Bauhaus* Weimar 1919-1923, Weimar and Munich 1923, p. 24.——*Paedagogisches Skizzenbuch*, Bauhausbuecher II, Munich 1925.—*Ueber die moderne Kunst* (speech at Jena 1924), Bern 1945.—Felix Klee. *Tagebuecher von Paul Klee*, Cologne 1956.——Juerg Spiller. *Paul Klee, Das bildnerische Denken, Nachgelassene Schriften zur Form- und Gestaltungslehre*, Basel and Stuttgart 1956.

BIBLIOGRAPHY: Leopold Zahn. *P. K.*, Potsdam 1920.——Wilhelm Hausenstein. *Kairuan oder eine Geschichte vom Maler Klee*, Munich 1921.—Will Grohmann. *P. K.*, Paris 1929.—René Crevel. *P. K.*, Paris 1930.—Will Grohmann. *P. K., Handzeichnungen 1921-1930*, Berlin 1934.—James Johnson Sweeney. *P. K.*, New York 1941.—James Thrall Soby. *The Prints of P. K.*, New York 1945.—*Cahiers d'Art* 20/21 (1945-1946).—Herbert Read, *P. K.*, London 1948.—Douglas Cooper. *P. K.*, London 1949.—Daniel Henry Kahnweiler. *P. K.*, Paris, New York 1950.—Werner Haftmann. *P. K.*, Munich 1950.—Carola Giedion-Welcker. *P. K.*, London 1952, Stuttgart 1954.—Will Grohmann. *P. K.*, Stuttgart 1954.—Hans Konrad Röthel. *P. K.* Wiesbaden 1955.—P. Courthion. *P. K.*, Feldafing 1955.—Grohmann, Gropius, Soupanet, *Paul Klee, mit*

Texten von ihm selbst, Feldafing 1956.—*Ausstellungskatalog*, Bern 1956.

OSKAR KOKOSCHKA

Born March 1, 1886 at Poechlarn on the Danube, Austria; lives at Villeneuve, Switzerland.

Originally intended to become a chemist. Studied art in Vienna with B. Loeffler at the School of Arts and Crafts of the Austrian Museum for Art and Industry. 1908-1914 stays in Vienna, Switzerland, and Berlin, where he joined the *Sturm*. Was wounded in the First World War. 1917 moved to Dresden. 1920-1924 Professor at the Dresden Academy. 1924 sudden resignation from his position. Travels in Europe and North Africa. 1931-1934 Vienna; 1934-1938 Prague. 1938 emigration to London. 1948-1949 prolonged stay in Italy. 1950 London (*Prometheus Saga* for Antoine Count Seilern). Since 1953 at Villeneuve on Lake Geneva. Every summer " School of Seeing "—an international summer course for plastic art in Salzburg.

OWN WRITINGS: *Schriften* 1907-1955, edited by Hans Maria Wingler, Munich 1956

BIBLIOGRAPHY: Paul Westheim. *O. K.*, Berlin 1918.——Georg Biermann. *O. K.*, Leipzig 1928.—Hans Heilmaier. *O. K.*, Paris 1929.—*Ausstellung Staedtische Galerie Mannheim*, 1931.—Thomas Mann. " *O. K.*," in *Der Wiener Kunstwanderer*, November 1933.—Hans Platschek. *O. K.*, Buenos Aires 1946.—Edith Hoffmann. *K., Life and Work*. London 1947.——James S. Plaut. *O. K.*, Boston and London 1948.—Michelangelo Maiciotto. *K.*, Florence 1949.—F. W. Arntz. *Verzeichnis des graphischen Werks*, exhibition catalogue Munich 1950.——Hans Maria Wingler. *O. K., Ein Lebensbild in zeitgenoessischen Dokumenten*, Munich 1956.—Hans Maria Wingler. *O. K.*, Salzburg 1956.

Paul Klee Plants
Drawing, 1920

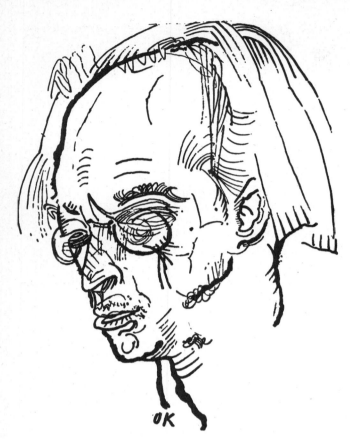

Oskar Kokoschka Herwarth Walden
Drawing, 1910

AUGUST MACKE

Born January 3, 1887 at Meschede on the Ruhr; killed in action September 26, 1914 near Perthes in the Champagne, France.

1904-1905 studied at the Duesseldorf Academy, then at the Duesseldorf School of Arts and Crafts with Ehmke. 1907 first journey to Paris, with Bernhard Koehler, the uncle of his future wife. During the winter, in Berlin studying with Corinth. 1908 second journey to Paris. 1909-1910 at Tegernsee. In contact with the New Artists' Association, Munich. Friendship with Marc. On the staff of the *Blaue Reiter* Almanac. Participation in their exhibition. 1912 Bonn. Participation in the *Sonderbund* exhibition in Cologne. In September, together with Marc, visit to Delaunay. 1913 for eight months at Lake Thun, Switzerland. April 1914 to Tunisia with Klee and Moilliet. Drafted into the army in August.

OWN WRITINGS: Contribution to *Im Kampf um die Kunst*, Antwort auf den Protest deutscher Kuenstler, Munich 1911, p. 80.—"Die Masken," in *Der Blaue Reiter*, Munich 1912, p. 21. Complete list *see* Vriesen.

BIBLIOGRAPHY: Walter Bombe. "A. M.," in *Das Kunstblatt* II (1918), p. 97.—Lothar Erdmann and Elisabeth Erdmann-Macke. *A. M., Zeichnungen*, First Series, Bonn 1919.—Walter Cohen. *A. M.*, Leipzig 1922.—Matthias Rech. "*Erinnerungen an A. M. aus dem Fruehjahr 1914*," in *Wallraf-Richartz-Jahrbuch* (1925), p. 213.—Lother Erdmann. *A. M., Die Unvergessenen*, edited by Ernst Juenger, Berlin 1928.—*Ausstellungskatalog der Kestner - Gesellschaft*, Hanover 1935.—*Gedaechtnis - Ausstellung Koeln 1947.*—Hermann Buenemann. "A. M.," in *Die Kunst* 48 (1950), p. 1.—Gustav Vriesen. *A. M.*, Stuttgart 1953 (with extensive bibliography).

FRANZ MARC

Born February 8, 1880 in Munich; killed in action, March 4, 1916 at Verdun, France.

Studied philosophy and theology at Munich University first, then studied with Hackl and Wilhelm von Diez the Munich Academy in order to become a painter. 1903 journey to France without any immediate artistic result. 1907 first marriage. On the evening of the wedding day alone to Paris. In 1910 he settled at Sindelsdorf, Upper Bavaria; friendship with Macke and acquaintance with Bernhard Koehler, who gave him 200 marks a month to be set off against pictures. 1911 marriage with Maria Franck, who became the trustee of his work after his death. 1911 member of the New Artists' Association, which he left in November to found the *Blaue Reiter*. The group's first exhibition was followed by the Almanac. 1913 participation in the organization of the First German Autumn Salon in Berlin. 1912, with Macke to Paris to visit Delaunay. 1914 moved to Ried near Benediktbeuren. Then military service.

OWN WRITINGS: Various Essays in *Pan*, *Sturm*, and in the *Blaue Reiter.—Briefe, Aufzeichnungen und Aphorismen*, Volume I, Berlin 1920.—*Briefe aus dem Feld*, Berlin 1940, and Stollhamm (Oldenburg) 1948.—*Aufzeichnungen und Aphorismen*, Galerie Guenther Franke, Munich 1946. Complete list of publications *see* Klaus Lankheit. *Ausstellungskatalog*, Moderne Galerie Otto Stangl, Munich 1949.

BIBLIOGRAPHY: Elisabeth Waib. *F. M.*, Frankfort on the Main 1933.—Alois J. Schardt. *F. M.*, Berlin (1936).—Hermann Buenemann. *F. M.*, *Aquarelle und Zeichnungen*, Munich 1948.—H. Demisch. *F, M., der Maler eines Neubeginns*, Berlin-Hanover 1948.—Klaus Lankheit. *F. M.*, Berlin 1950.—Maria Marc and Georg Schmidt. *F. M.*, *Botschaften an den Prinzen Jussuff*, Munich 1954.

August Macke Greeting Woodcut
State Collection of Graphic Art, Munich

GEORG MEISTERMANN

Born June 16, 1911 at Solingen; lives in Duesseldorf as teacher at the Academy.

1929-1933 studied at the Duesseldorf Academy with Heuser, Nauen, and Mataré. 1937-1939 travels in France, Holland, and England. 1949 First Prize at the Blevin Davies Competition. 1933 appointed to the Staedel School of Art, Frankfort on the Main. Since 1955 in Duesseldorf.

BIBLIOGRAPHY: O. Domnick. *Die schoepferischen Kraefte in der abstrakten Malerei*, Bergen 1947.

PAULA MODERSOHN-BECKER

Born February 8, 1876 in Dresden; died November 21, 1907 at Worpswede.

Grew up in Bremen, whereto her family had moved in 1888. 1893-1895 studied to become a teacher. 1896-1898 studied in Berlin. 1898 for the first time at Worpswede under Mackensen. Winter 1899-1900 in Paris with Clara Westhoff, working at the Académie Colarossi and at the École des Beaux-Arts. 1903 marriage with the painter Otto Modersohn. Friendship with Rilke. 1903, 1905, and 1906 back in Paris, friendship with Bernhard Hoetger.

OWN WRITINGS: *Briefe und Tagebuecher*, edited by S. D. Gallwitz, Hanover 1917.

Franz Marc Tiger Woodcut, 1912
State Collection of Graphic Art, Munich

BIBLIOGRAPHY: Rainer Maria Rilke. *Worpswede*, Leipzig 1903.—Rainer Maria Rilke. *Requiem, Fuer eine Freundin*, Leipzig 1909.—Curt Stoermer. *P. M.-B.*, Katalog ihrer Werke I, Worpswede 1913 (not continued).—Gustav Pauli. *P. M.-B.*, Leipzig 1919.—W. Mueller-Wulckow. *Die P. M.-B. Sammlung von Ludwig Roselius*, Bremen 1927.—Rolf Hetsch. *P. M.-B.*, Berlin (1932).

OTTO MUELLER

Born October 16, 1874 at Liebau, Silesia; died September 24, 1930 in Breslau.

His father was an officer, his mother probably a deserted gypsy child who had been brought up in the family of Gerhart Hauptmann. Apprenticeship in a lithographer's workshop after having attended the elementary school; 1895-1898 at the Dresden Academy. 1898-1907 stay in the Riesengebirge. 1908 Berlin, meeting with Erich Heckel. 1910 member of the Artists' Community *Bruecke*. 1915-1918 military service. 1919 Professor at the Breslau Academy.

BIBLIOGRAPHY: Paul Westheim. " O. M.," in *Das Kunstblatt* II (1918), p. 129.—Karl Scheffler. " O. M.," in *Kunst und Kuenstler* XVII (1919), p. 349.—*Ausstellungskatalog* of the " Bruecke," Bern 1948.—Eberhard Troeger. *O. M.*, Freiburg in Breisgau 1949.—*Ausstellungskatalog O. M.*, Kestner-Gesellschaft, Hanover 1956.

GABRIELE MUENTER

Born February 19, 1877 in Berlin, lives at Murnau.

Early youth spent in Westphalia, Coblenz, and travelling in the U.S.A. 1901-1902 School of the Munich Association of Female Artists with Angelo Jank. 1902 at the " Phalanx," first with Huesgen in the modelling class, then with Kandinsky. 1904-1908 journeys with Kandinsky to Holland, Tunisia, Dresden, Belgium, Rapallo, Paris, Switzerland, Berlin, Upper Bavaria, and Salzkammergut. 1908 with Kandinsky to Murnau on Staffelsee, Upper Bavaria, where she still lives in the same house. 1909 charter member of the New Artists' As-

Franz Marc Gambolling Foals Woodcut, 1912
State Collection of Graphic Art, Munich

sociation, Munich. November 1911, resignation, together with Kandinsky and Marc, and exhibition of the *Blaue Reiter*. 1913 participation in the First German Autumn Salon, Berlin. 1914 with Kandinsky to Switzerland. 1915 dissolution of the joint household with Kandinsky in Munich. 1915 with Kandinsky to Stockholm. Termination of their communal life after Kandinsky's return to Moscow, spring 1916. 1918-1928 Copenhagen. 1920-1927 travels to Munich, Murnau, Cologne, Berlin, Ticino, and Engadin. 1929-1930 France. Since 1931, with few interruptions, permanently at Murnau.

OWN WRITINGS: " Bekenntnisse und Erinnerungen," in Hartlaub, G. F., *Menschenbilder*.

BIBLIOGRAPHY: G. F. Hartlaub. *G. M., Menschenbilder in Zeichnungen*, Berlin 1952.—*Ausstellungskatalog*, Munich 1952, with an introduction by Johannes Eichner.

Emil Nolde Family Woodcut, 1917
State Collection of Graphic Art, Munich

Gabriele Muenter " Kandinsky "
Woodcut, 1907

ERNST WILHELM NAY

Born June 11, 1902 in Berlin; lives in Cologne.

1925-1928 studied with Hofer in Berlin. 1928 Paris, first influence of Picasso. 1930 Rome Prize. 1936 and 1937 in Norway on Edvard Munch's invitation. Lofoten Islands pictures. 1939-1944 war service. Small water colours in Brittany. 1945 Hofheim in the Taunus. Since 1951 in Cologne.

OWN WRITINGS: *Aphorismen*, exhibition catalogue Guenther Franke, Munich 1953. -*Vom Gestaltwert der Farbe*, Munich 1955.

BIBLIOGRAPHY: *Katalog der Kestner-Gesellschaft*, Hanover 1950.—Will Grohmann. " E. W. N.," in *Cahiers d'Art 27* (1952), p. 219.—Walter Hess. " Der Maler E. W. N.," in *Die Kunst 54* (1956), p. 248.—Fritz Usinger. *E. W. N., Aquarelle*, Munich 1956.

EMIL NOLDE

Born August 7, 1867 at Nolde, North Schleswig; died April 31, 1956 at Seebuell near Niebuell, Schleswig.

1885-1889 at the Sauermann School of Carving and the Vocational School at Flensburg. 1892-1898 teacher at the St. Gallen Technical School (Switzerland). From 1898 free-lance painter. He had earned enough money by postcards with mountain outlines to finish his studies. Journeys to Munich, Paris, and Copenhagen. From 1902 on mainly in Berlin. After 1904 he called himself Nolde, his real surname was Hansen. 1905-1907 stay in Dresden, contacts with the *Bruecke*. 1910 Hamburg, 1913 journey to Russia, Siberia, Japan, 1914 back to Germany via the South Seas. 1936 forbidden to work. 1939-1942 during the summer months mainly at Seebuell, in the winter in Berlin. From 1942 permanently at his home near Seebuell. Stopped painting 1952.

OWN WRITINGS: *Briefe* from the years 1894-1926, edited by Max Sauerlandt, Berlin 1927.—*Das eigene Leben*, Berlin 1931.—*Jahre der Kaempfe*, Berlin 1934.

BIBLIOGRAPHY: G. Schiefler. *Das Graphische Werk E. N.'s*, Volume I, Berlin 1911, Volume II, Berlin 1927.—Max Sauer-

Otto Mueller Girl in Landscape
Woodcut

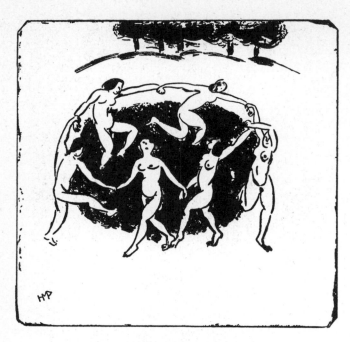

Max Pechstein Dance Etching, 1917
State Collection of Graphic Art, Munich

landt. " E. N.," in *Zeitschrift fuer Bildende Kunst* XXV (1914), p. 181.—Theodor Daeubler. "E. N.," in *Das Kunstblatt* I (1917), p. 114.—Hans Fehr. " Aus Leben und Werkstatt E. N.'s, in *Das Kunstblatt* III (1919), p. 205.—Max Sauerlandt. *E. N.*, Berlin 1922.—*Festschrift fuer Emil Nolde* (with contributions by Klee, Sauerlandt, Schiefler and others), Dresden 1927.—P. F. Schmidt. *E. N.*. Leipzig 1929.—Hans Holtorf. *Sommerwolken. Ein Geburtstagsgruss an E. N.*, Der Dreiklang, Flensburg 1947.—Hans Fehr. " E. N. zum 80. Geburtstag," in *Der Kleine Bund* No. 32, Bern 1947.—Hans Fehr. " E. N. als Lehrer in St. Gallen," in *Das Bodenseejahrbuch*, Zurich 1947.

MAX PECHSTEIN

Born January 31, 1881 at Eckersbach near Zwickau; died June 25, 1955 in Berlin.

1896 apprenticeship with a house-painter. 1900 at the Dresden School of Arts and Crafts, and the Academy. Work in the architectural studio of Wilhelm Kreis. 1906 met Heckel and Kirchner, membership in the *Bruecke*. 1907 trip to Italy. From 1908 on in Berlin, spending most of the summers at Nidden, East Prussia. As the most conventional among the *Bruecke* artists he was the first to be successful. 1910 charter member of the Berlin New Secession. 1914 journey to the Palau Islands. 1916-1917 soldier. 1919 back in Berlin. 1922 member of the Berlin Academy of Fine Arts; blackballed in 1934. 1940-1945 on the Pomeranian coast. After the war teacher at the Academy of Fine Arts in Berlin.

OWN WRITINGS: " Gedichte und Aufzeichnungen," in Paul Westheim. *Kuenstlerbekenntnisse*, Berlin (1925).—*Ruf an die Jugend*, Aussaat, Stuttgart 1946.

BIBLIOGRAPHY: Max Osborn. *M. P.*, Berlin 1922.—Paul Fechter. *Das Graphische Werk M. P.'s*, Berlin 1921 (with catalogue).—Georg Biermann. " M. P.," in *Junge Kunst*, Volume I, Leipzig 1919.—Walter Heymann. *M. P.*, Munich 1916.—Konrad Lemmer. *M. P. und der Beginn des Expressionismus*, Berlin 1949.

HANS PURRMANN

Born April 10, 1880 at Speyer; lives at Montagnola, Switzerland.

Apprenticeship as a house-painter. 1898-1900 studied at the Karlsruhe School of Arts and Crafts. 1900-1905 at the Munich Academy with Hackl and Stuck. 1906-1914 in Paris with Matisse, from 1908 as " *massier* " (shop steward) at his school. Organized several Matisse exhibitions in Germany. 1914-1916 Beilstein in Wuerttemberg. 1916-1921 Berlin. Travels to Italy and France. 1935 Director of Villa Romana, Florence. 1943 moved to Lugano.

OWN WRITINGS: " Aus der Werkstatt Henri Matisses," in *Kunst und Kuenstler* XX (1922), p. 167.—Various art criticisms from the years 1928-1933.—" Ueber Henri Matisse," in *Das Werk* 33 (1946), p. 185.—" Erinnerungen an meine Studienzeit," in *Das Werk* 34 (1947), p. 366.—" Die Einheit des Kunstwerks," in *Das Werk* 36 (1949), No. 5, reprinted in the catalogue of the travelling exhibition 1950.

BIBLIOGRAPHY: Edmund Hausen. *Der Maler H. P.*, Berlin 1950.

CHRISTIAN ROHLFS

Born January 22, 1849 at Niendorf near Leezen, Holstein; died January 8, 1938 at Hagen.

Youngest son of a smallholder and heir to the farm. 1864 injured by a fall from a tree, and therefore no longer eligible as heir. 1869 to Berlin with a recommendation from Theodor Storm, then to the Weimar Academy. In the eighties, tendency towards Impressionism; about 1900 change towards

Schmidt-Rottluff Girl from Kowno
Woodcut, 1915. State Collection of Graphic Art, Munich

Expressionism. 1901 appointed to the Folkwang School at Hagen by Karl Ernst Osthaus. 1905 beginning of friendship with Nolde. After 1911 predominantly pictures in tempera and mixed techniques. From 1927 on extensive stays each year in Ascona. 1937 blackballed from the Prussian Academy of Fine Arts.

BIBLIOGRAPHY: Hans Tintelnot. *Einleitung zum Katalog der Wanderausstellung zum 100. Geburtstag*, Goettingen 1949.——Paul Vogt. *C. R.*, Oeuvre Katalog der Druckgraphik, p. 1, 1950.—Gertrud Bender. " *C. R.*, ein Mittler zwischen zwei Jahrhunderten," in *Westfalen* 30 (1952), p. 1.—*Ausstellungs-katalog 1955*, introduction by Walter Ueberwasser.—Helene Rohlfs and Paul Vogt. *Blaetter aus Ascona*, Munich 1955.——Paul Vogt. *C. R.*, Cologne 1956.

OSKAR SCHLEMMER

Born September 4, 1888 in Stuttgart; died April 13, 1943 at Baden-Baden.

Studied at the Stuttgart Academy with Hoelzel, co-operation with Baumeister and Meyer-Amden. 1910 Berlin. 1911 Stuttgart. 1920 teacher at the *Bauhaus* in Weimar, later in Dessau. 1922 performance of his *Triadic Ballet* in Stuttgart. 1929-1932 Professor at the Breslau Academy. 1932 teacher at the Berlin Academy. Dismissed in 1933. Lived thereafter in rural solitude, first at Eichberg, South Baden, from 1937 on at Schringen near Badenweiler. 1940 position at Herbert's Institute of Painting Technique at Wuppertal.

OWN WRITINGS: " Paul Klee und die Stuttgarter Akademie," in *Das Kunstblatt* IV (1920), p. 123.—*Die Buehne im Bauhaus*, Staatliches Bauhaus Weimar 1919-1925, Weimar and Munich 1925.—" Alte Oper – neue Oper," in *Das Kunstblatt* XIV (1930), p. 242.—*Meyer-Amden*, Zurich 1934.

BIBLIOGRAPHY: Franz Roh, *O. S., Die Kunst des 20. Jahr-hunderts*, Munich 1947.—Hans Hildebrandt. *O. S.*, Munich 1952.

KARL SCHMIDT-ROTTLUFF

Born December 1, 1884 at Rottluff near Chemnitz; lives in Berlin.

1905 graduated from high school. 1905-1906 architectural studies with Fritz Schumacher at the Dresden Institute of Technology. Founded, together with Kirchner and Heckel, the Artists' Community *Bruecke*, 1905. During the summer months usually at Dangast, East Prussia. Since fall 1911 in Berlin, where he met Otto Mueller. 1915-1918 war service in Russia. From 1919 on, summer on the Kuhrische Nehrung in Holstein or in Pomerania. 1923 Italy, together with the sculptors Kolbe and Scheibe. 1925 Dalmatia. 1926 Paris, 1927 and 1929 Ticino. 1930 at the German Academy in Rome. 1932-1942 during spring usually in the Taunus. 1936 forbidden to exhibit, later to work, by the National Socialists. Since 1946 Professor at the Academy of Fine Arts in Berlin.

OWN WRITINGS: " Brief ueber Munch und die *Bruecke*," in *Die Schanze* I (1951), p. 5.

BIBLIOGRAPHY: Ludwig Coellen. " K. S.-R.," in *Das Kunstblatt* I (1917), p. 321.—Eckart von Sydow. " S.-R.," in *Der Cicerone* X (1912), p. 75.—Ernst Gosebruch. " S.-R.," in *Genius* II (1920), p. 5.—Karl Scheffler, " K. S.-R.," in *Kunst und Kuenstler* XVIII (1920), p. 274.—M. R. Valentiner. *K. S.-R.*, Leipzig 1920.—Rosa Schapire. *K. S.-R.'s Graphisches Werk*, Berlin 1924.—Will Grohmann. *K. S.-R.*, Stuttgart 1956 (with extensive bibliography).

Christian Rohlfs Crouching Nude
Woodcut

ERNST WEIERS

Born September 17, 1909 at Oespel, Westphalia; lives at Bernried on Starnberg Lake, Upper Bavaria.

Comes from peasant stock, was brought up by Jesuits, and discovered art through his meeting with Christian Rohlfs. Helped by Edvard Munch, Schmidt-Rottluff, and Ludwig Gies. 1930-1933 studied at the Duesseldorf Academy with Campendonk and Klee. Took refuge, 1933, in a mountain hut in the Ticino. 1939-1945 war service; prisoner of war in Russia till 1948. 1956 Art Prize of Boettcherstrasse, Bremen, for *Day and Night*, a portfolio with 10 coloured lithographs.

BIBLIOGRAPHY: Hans Konrad Roethel. " E. W.," in *Die Kunst* 51 (1953), p. 441.

FRITZ WINTER

Born September 22, 1905 at Altenboegge, Westphalia; living since 1935 at Diessen on Ammersee, Upper Bavaria; Professor at the Cassel Academy.

Oldest son of a miner's large family. After visiting the elementary school, temporary pupil at the grammar school. Trained as an electrician in the mines, then worked as a miner. 1926 hiked through Holland. 1927 admitted to the *Bauhaus*, Dessau. 1930 *Bauhaus* Diploma. 1931 Halle on Saale. 1933 Karlsfeld-Allach near Munich. After 1933, under the National Socialist oppression, he often worked as an artisan. 1939-1945 war service, prisoner of war in Russia till 1949.

BIBLIOGRAPHY: Ernst Kallai. " Zu den Arbeiten von F. W.," in *Die neue Stadt*, May 1932, p. 42.—Schreiber-Rueffer. " F. W., ein Malerphilosoph," in *Forum* 7 (1937).—Schreiber-Rueffer. " F. W.," in O. Domnick, *Die schoepferischen Kraefte in der abstrakten Malerei*, Bergen 1947.—Werner Haftmann. *F. W.*, Bern 1951.—Will Grohmann. " F. W.," in *Cahiers d'Art* 28 (1953), p. 141.—Harro Ernst, " F. W.'s Beitrag zum Thema Abstraktion," in *Die Kunst* 54 (1956), p. 330.

Willi Baumeister Drawing
1932

BIBLIOGRAPHY

I am greatly indebted to Hans Beilhack, Munich, for his help in compiling the bibliography.

1893 ADOLF HILDEBRAND, *Das Problem der Form*, Strasbourg.

1896 AUGUST ENDELL, *Um die Schönheit*, Munich.

1900 SIGMUND FREUD, *Traumdeutung*, Vienna.
GUSTAV PAULI, *Kunsturtheil und Kunstgefühl*, Bremen.

1901 *Die Insel der Blödsinnigen*. Die Tollheiten der Moderne in Wort und Bild, edited by L. Wulff, Berlin.

1903 HERMANN OBRIST, *Neue Möglichkeiten in der bildenden Kunst*, Jena.

1906 OSKAR BIE, *Was ist moderne Kunst?* Berlin.

1907 HUGO VON REININGHAUS, *Entwicklungsgeschichte der modernen Malerei*, Munich.
WILHELM WORRINGER, *Abstraktion und Einfühlung*, Munich.

1909 ALFRED KUBIN, *Die andere Seite*, novel, Munich.

1910 SIGMUND FREUD, *Über Psychoanalyse*, Vienna.
WILHELM NIEMEYER, *Denkschrift des Sonderbundes* Düsseldorf.
HUGO VON REININGHAUS, *Demarkationslinien der modernen Kunst*. Munich.

1911 THEODOR ALT, *Die Herabwertung der deutschen Kunst durch die Parteigänger des Impressionismus*, Mannheim.
Ein Protest deutscher Künstler, with an introduction by CARL VINNEN, Jena.
Im Kampf um die Kunst. Antwort auf den Protest deutscher Künstler (with contributions by Kandinsky, Liebermann, Macke, Marc, Pechstein, Uhde and others), Munich. Second edition 1913 under the title *Deutsche und französische Kunst*.
HERBERT EULENBERG, *Die Kunst in unserer Zeit*, Eine Trauerrede an die deutsche Nation, Leipzig.
W. HELLPACH, *Das Pathologische in der modernen Kunst*, Heidelberg.

1912 E. W. BREDT, *Häßliche Kunst?*, Munich.
LUDWIG COELLEN, *Die neue Malerei*, Munich.
THEODOR DÄUBLER, *Der neue Standpunkt*, Dresden-Hellerau.
CARL EINSTEIN, *Negerplastik*, Leipzig.
OTTO FISCHER, *Das neue Bild*. Publication of the New Artists' Association Munich, Munich.
WASSILY KANDINSKY, *Über das Geistige in der Kunst*, Munich.

1913 WILHELM VON BODE, *Die "neue Kunst"* in Der Kunstfreund, Berlin.
MAX BROD, *Über die Schönheit häßlicher Bilder*, Leipzig.
FRITZ BURGER, *Cézanne und Hodler*, Introduction into Painting of Today, Munich.
JULIUS MEIER-GRAEFE, *Wohin treiben wir?* Two Speeches on Art and Civilization, Berlin.
MAX RAPHAEL (Schönlanck), *Von Monet zu Picasso*, Munich.

EMIL UTITZ, *Die Grundlagen der jüngsten Kunstbewegung*, Principles of Aesthetics and Development of Modern Painting, Stuttgart.
HERWARTH WALDEN, *Deutscher Herbstsalon*, Berlin.

1914 HERMANN BAHR, *Expressionismus*, Munich.
A. I. EDDY, *Cubists and Post-Impressionism*, Chicago.
PAUL FECHTER, *Der Expressionismus*, Munich.
WILHELM HAUSENSTEIN, *Die Bildende Kunst der Gegenwart*, Stuttgart and Berlin.
WILHELM HAUSENSTEIN, *Vom Künstler und seiner Seele*, Heidelberg.
JULIUS MEIER-GRAEFE, *Entwicklungsgeschichte der modernen Kunst*, 2nd revised and supplemented edition, Munich.

1915 ADOLF BEHNE, *Zur neuen Kunst*, Berlin.
MAX PICARD, *Expressionistische Bauernmalerei*, Munich.

1916 MAX LIEBERMANN, *Die Phantasie in der Malerei*, Berlin.
MAX PICARD, *Das Ende des Impressionismus*, Munich.

1917 FRITZ BURGER, *Einführung in die moderne Kunst*, Berlin.
SIGMUND FREUD, *Vorlesungen zur Einführung in die Psychoanalyse*, Vienna.
HERWARTH WALDEN, *Einblick in die Kunst*, Expressionism, Futurism, Cubism, Berlin.
ALFRED WERNER, *Impressionismus und Eexpressionismus*, Leipzig and Frankfort.

1918 KASIMIR EDSCHMID, *Über den Expressionismus in der Literatur und die neue Dichtung*, Dresden-Hellerau.
WILHELM HAUSENSTEIN, *Über den Expressionismus in der Malerei*, Berlin.
CARL GEORG HEISE, *Die Sammlung des Freiherrn A. v. d. Heydt*, Leipzig.
WILHELM WAETZOLDT, *Deutsche Malerei seit 1870*, Leipzig.
HERWARTH WALDEN, *Expressionismus*. Die Kunstwende, Berlin.

1919 *Ja! Stimmen des Arbeitsrats für Kunst in Berlin*, Berlin.
OTTO BRAIN, *Studien zum Expressionismus*. Zeitschrift für Ästhetik und Allgemeine Kunstwissenschaft XIII (I/1919).
THEODOR DÄUBLER, *Im Kampf um die moderne Kunst*, Berlin.
OTTO GRAUTOFF, *Formzertrümmerung und Formaufbau in der bildenden Kunst*, Berlin.
GUSTAV FRIEDRICH HARTLAUB, *Kunst und Religion*, Leipzig.
KARL ERNST OSTHAUS, *Grundzüge der Stilentwicklung*, Hagen.
KARL SCHEFFLER, *Die Zukunft der deutschen Kunst*, Berlin.
HERWARTH WALDEN, *Die neue Malerei*, Berlin.
PAUL WESTHEIM, *Die Welt als Vorstellung*, Berlin.
K. VON ZIESCHÉ, *Expressionismus*. Warendorf.

1920 *Schöpferische Konfession*. With contributions by Klee, Marc, Pechstein and others, Berlin.
GUSTAV FRIEDRICH HARTLAUB, *Die neue deutsche Graphik*, Berlin.

WILHELM HAUSENSTEIN, *Die Kunst in diesem Augenblick*, Munich.

PAUL HERRMANN, *Diktatur in der modernen Kunst*, Berlin.

HANS HILDEBRANDT, *Der Expressionismus in der Malerei*, Stuttgart and Berlin.

RICHARD HUELSENBECK, *En avant Dada*, A History of Dadaism, Hanover.

PAUL ERICH KÜPPERS, *Der Kubismus, ein Formproblem unserer Zeit*, Leipzig.

FRIEDRICH MÄRKER, *Lebensgefühl und Weltgefühl*, Munich.

KURT PFISTER, *Deutsche Graphiker der Gegenwart*, Leipzig.

OSKAR PFISTER, *Der psychologische und biologische Untergrund expressionistischer Bilder*, Bern and Leipzig.

ECKART VON SYDOW, *Die deutsche expressionistische Kultur und Malerei*, Berlin.

1921 MAX DERI, *Die neue Malerei*, Leipzig.

OTTO GRAUTOFF, *Die neue Kunst*, Berlin.

LUDWIG JUSTI, *Neue Kunst*, Berlin.

FRANZ LANDSBERGER, *Impressionismus und Expressionismus*, Leipzig.

GEORG MARZYNSKI, *Die Methode des Expressionismus*, Leipzig.

MAX RAPHAEL (Schönlanck), *Idee und Gestalt*, Munich.

ECKART VON SYDOW, *Die Kultur der Dekadenz*, Dresden.

ITALO TAVOLATO, *Espressionismo*, Valori Plastici III (1921), Rome.

PAUL WESTHEIM, *Das Holzschnittbuch*, Potsdam.

WILHELM WORRINGER, *Künstlerische Zeitfragen*, Munich.

1922 CURT GLASER, *Graphik der Neuzeit*, Berlin.

GUSTAV FRIEDRICH HARTLAUB, *Der Genius im Kinde*, Breslau.

KARL JASPERS, *Strindberg und van Gogh*, Leipzig.

HANS PRINZHORN, *Bildnerei der Geisteskranken*, Berlin.

E. W. SINGER, *Die Graphik der Neuzeit*, Berlin.

HANS VON WEDDERKOP, *Deutsche Graphik des Westens*, Weimar.

1923 OSKAR BEYER, *Welt-Kunst*, About the Changing Evaluation of Art History, Dresden.

WALTER LURJE, *Mystisches Denken*, Insanity and Modern Art, Stuttgart.

JULIUS MEIER-GRAEFE, *Die Kunst der Gegenwart*, 42 Water Colours and Drawings, Munich.

W. PAULCKE, *Steinzeitkunst und moderne Kunst – ein Vergleich*, Stuttgart.

PAUL FERDINAND SCHMIDT, *Kunst der Gegenwart*, Berlin. *Staatliches Bauhaus*, Weimar 1919-1923, Munich.

PAUL WESTHEIM, *Für und Wider*, Potsdam.

1924 HANS HILDEBRANDT, *Die Kunst des 19. und 20. Jahrhunderts*, Potsdam.

1925 ADOLF BEHNE, *Von Kunst zur Gestaltung*, Introduction into Modern Painting, Berlin.

EL LISSITZKY und HANS ARP, *Die Kunstismen*, Zurich, Munich, Leipzig.

GEORGE GROSZ und WIELAND HERZFELDE, *Die Kunst ist in Gefahr*, Berlin.

RICHARD HAMANN, *Die deutsche Malerei vom Rokoko bis zum Expressionismus*, Leipzig.

ROM LANDAU, *Der unbestechliche Minos*, Criticism of the Art of Today, Hamburg.

FRANZ ROH, *Nach-Expressionismus. Magischer Realismus*, Leipzig.

HANS TIETZE, *Lebendige Kunstwissenschaft*, The Crisis of Art and Art History, Vienna.

PAUL WESTHEIM, *Künstlerbekenntnisse*, Berlin.

1926 CARL EINSTEIN, *Die Kunst des zwanzigsten Jahrhunderts*, Berlin.

ERNST KROPP, *Wandlung der Form im 20. Jahrhundert*, Berlin.

KARL SCHEFFLER, *Geschichte der europäischen Kunst im 19. Jahrhundert*, Berlin.

1927 HUGO BALL, Die *Flucht aus der Zeit*, Munich.

KURT BREYSIG, *Eindruckskunst und Ausdruckskunst*, Berlin.

H. KRÖLLER-MÜLLER, *Die Entwicklung der modernen Malerei*, Leipzig.

K. MALEWITSCH, *Die gegenstandslose Welt*, Bauhausbücher XI, Munich.

EMIL UTITZ, *Die Überwindung des Expressionismus*, Stuttgart.

KARL WOERMANN, *Geschichte der Kunst aller Zeiten und Völker*, Volume VI, Leipzig.

1928 ANDRÉ BRETON, *Le Surréalisme et la Peinture*, Paris.

ECKART VON SYDOW, *Psychoanalyse und Kunstwissenschaft* in: H. PRINZHORN, *Auswirkungen der Psychoanalyse in Wissenschaft und Leben*, Leipzig.

1929 RICHARD BIE, *Deutsche Malerei der Gegenwart*, Weimar.

KARL SCHEFFLER, *L'art pour l'art*, Leipzig.

ECKART VON SYDOW, *Form und Symbol*, Potsdam.

1930 MAURICE CASTEELS, *Die Sachlichkeit in der modernen Kunst*, Paris.

JEAN FROIS-WITTMANN, *Moderne Kunst und Lustprinzip*, Versuch einer psychoanalytischen Rechtfertigung von Expressionismus und Surrealismus, in: Die Psychoanalytische Bewegung Volume XI, H. 3, 1930, pag. 211.

MARGHERITA G. SARFATTI, *Storia della Pittura Moderna*, Rome.

LOTHAR SCHREYER, *Die bildende Kunst der Deutschen*, Hamburg.

EMILE WALDMANN, *La peinture allemande contemporaine*, Paris.

1931 ALFRED H. BARR, *German Painting and Sculpture*, New York.

LUDWIG JUSTI, *Von Corinth bis Klee*, Berlin.

1932 HERMANN KLUMPP, *Abstraktion in der Malerei*, Berlin.

PAUL SCHULTZE-NAUMBURG, *Kampf um die Kunst*, Munich.

1933 HEDWIG GOLLOB, *Entwicklungsgeschichte der modernen Kunst*, Strasbourg.

HERBERT READ, *Art Now*, London.

1934 HANS WEIGERT, *Die Kunst von heute als Spiegel der Zeit*, Leipzig.

1935 RENÉ HUYGHE and GERMAIN BAZIN, *Histoire de l'Art Contemporain*, La Peinture, Paris.

MAX SAUERLANDT, *Die Kunst der letzten dreißig Jahre*, edited by HARALD BUSCH, Berlin.

FRITZ SCHMALENBACH, *Jugendstil*, Würzburg.

PAUL SCHULTZE-NAUMBURG, *Kunst und Rasse*, Munich.

1936 HERBERT READ, *Surrealism*, London.

1937 ALFRED H. BARR, *Fantastic Art, Dada, Surrealism*, Museum of Modern Art, New York.

BRUNO KROLL, *Deutsche Malerei der Gegenwart*, Berlin.

WOLFGANG WILLRICH, *Die Säuberung des Kunsttempels*, A Polemical Paper for the Recovery of German Art in the Nordic Spirit, Munich and Berlin.

1938 HERBERT BAYER, *Bauhaus 1919-1928*, New York.

ADOLF DRESLER, *Deutsche Kunst und entartete " Kunst,"* Munich.

PETER THOENE, *Modern German Art*. Foreword by HERBERT READ, London.

CHRISTIAN ZERVOS, *Histoire de l'art contemporain*, Paris.

1939 *Art in Our Time*, Museum of Modern Art, New York.

B. CHAMPIGNEULLE, *L'inquiétude dans l'art d'aujourd'hui*, Paris.

Gemälde und Plastiken moderner Meister aus deutschen Museen, auction catalogue of Galerie Fischer of June 30, 1939, Lucerne.

1941 FRIEDRICH AHLERS-HESTERMANN, *Stilwende*, Awakening of the Youth around 1900, Berlin.

FRITZ SCHMALENBACH, *Grundlinien des Frühexpressionismus*, studies in Art History, Basel.

1943 WERNER RITTICH, *Deutsche Kunst der Gegenwart*, Breslau.

CARL GEORG HEISE, *Die Sammlung Bauer*, Berlin. Not for sale.

1944 *Art in Progress*, Museum of Modern Art, New York. *Documents of Modern Art*, edited by ROBERT MOTHERWELL, New York.

1945 MAURICE NADEAU, *Histoire du Surréalisme*, Paris. R. GOLDWATER and M. TREVES, *Artists on Art*, New York.

1946 ALFRED H. BARR, *What is Modern Painting?* New York.

HANS ECKSTEIN, *Maler und Bildhauer in München*, Munich.

1947 OTMAR DOMNICK, *Die schöpferischen Kräfte der abstrakten Malerei*, Stuttgart.

GUSTAV FRIEDRICH HARTLAUB, *Die Graphik des Expressionismus in Deutschland*, Stuttgart.

CURT VON LORCK, *Expressionismus*, Lübeck.

PETER MEYER, *Europäische Kunstgeschichte*, Zurich.

EMIL PREETORIUS, *Gedanken zur Kunst*, Munich.

1948 PIERRE BERÈS, *Cubism, Futurism, Dadaism, Expressionism and the Surrealist Movement in Literature and Art*, New York.

ROMANO GUARDINI, *Über des Wesen des Kunstwerks*, Tübingen.

ANDRÉ MALRAUX, *Psychologie de l'Art*, Geneva.

FRITZ MARTINI, *Was ist Expressionismus?* Urach.

MAURICE NADEAU, *Documents Surréalistes*, Paris.

FRITZ NEMITZ, *Deutsche Malerei der Gegenwart*, Munich.

MAX PICARD, *Die Welt des Schweigens*, Zurich.

S. RUDOLPH, *Die Krise der Kunst in Künstlerbriefen*, Lorch.

HENRY RUSSELL-HITCHCOCK, *Painting Toward Architecture*, New York.

HANS SEDLMAYR, *Verlust der Mitte*, Figurative Arts of the 19th Centuries as Symptom and Symbol of the Time, Salzburg.

JAMES THRALL SOBY, *Contemporary Painters*, New York.

GERHARD STRAUSS, *Dokumente zur " Entarteten Kunst "* in: *Festgabe an Karl Hofer*, Berlin.

WILHELM WORRINGER, *Problematik der Gegenwartskunst*, Munich.

1949 THEODOR W. ADORNO, *Philosophie der neuen Musik*, Tübingen.

GOTTFRIED BENN, *Ausdruckswelt*, Essays and Aphorisms, Wiesbaden.

MAX BURCHARTZ, *Gleichnis der Harmonie*, Munich.

JEAN GEBSER, *Ursprung und Gegenwart*, Stuttgart.

WERNER HAFTMANN, *Deutsche Maler*, Steinheim.

WILHELM HAUSENSTEIN, *Was bedeutet die moderne Kunst?*, Leutstetten near Munich.

MAURICE RAYNAL, *Histoire de la Peinture Moderne*, Geneva.

PAUL ORTWIN RAVE, *Kunst-Diktatur im Dritten Reich*, Hamburg.

RUDOLF SCHLICHTER, *Das Abenteuer der Kunst*, Hamburg.

MICHEL SEUPHOR, *L'Art abstrait*. Its Origins and First Masters, Paris.

WALTER WINKLER, *Psychologie der modernen Kunst* Tübingen.

1950 ALAIN BOSQUET, *Surrealismus 1924-1949*, Berlin.

JEAN CASSOU, *Situation de l'art moderne*, Paris.

MARTIN HEIDEGGER, *Holzwege*, Frankfort.

Geschichte der Modernen Malerei, Skira, Geneva.

DORIS WILD, *Moderne Malerei : Ihre Entwicklung seit dem Expressionismus*, Zurich.

DIETER WYSS, *Der Surrealismus*, Heidelberg.

1951 *Documents*. Numéro special: *L'Art allemand*, Offenburg.

KLAUS LANKHEIT, *Die Frühromantik und die Grundlagen der gegenstandslosen Malerei*, Neue Heidelberger Jahrbücher 1951, pag. 55, Heidelberg.

HENRY F. LENNING, *The Art Nouveau*, The Hague.

R. MOTHERWELL, *The Dada Painters and Poets*, New York.

P. REGAMEY, O. P., *La Querelle de l'art sacré*, Paris.

ALFRED STANGE. *Über die Einsamkeit der modernen Kunst*, Bonn.

1952 UMBRO APOLLONIO, *" Die Brücke " e la Cultura dell' Espressionismo*, Venice.

ALBRECHT FABRI, *Interview mit Sisyphos*, Cologne.

PAUL HASAERTS, *La Peinture expressioniste en Europe et en Flandre*, Les Arts Plastiques V, pag. 369, Brussels.

HERBERT READ, *The Philosophy of Modern Art*, London.

PAUL FERDINAND SCHMIDT, *Geschichte der modernen Malerei*, Stuttgart.

Témoignages pour l'Art Abstrait, edited by ALVARD, JULIEN and GINDERTAEL, Paris.

1953 WILL GROHMANN, *Bildende Kunst und Architektur*. Between the Wars, Volume III, Berlin.

WERNER HAFTMANN, *Deutsche abstrakte Maler*, Baden-Baden.

WALTER HESS, *Das Problem der Farbe in Selbstzeugnissen*, Munich.

1954 ALFRED H. BARR, *Masters of Modern Art*, Museum of Modern Art, New York.

CHRISTEL DENECKE, *Die Farbe im Expressionismus bei Franz Marc und Emil Nolde*, Düsseldorf.

LUDWIG GROTE, *Deutsche Kunst im 20. Jahrhundert*, Munich.

WERNER HAFTMANN, *Malerei im 20. Jahrhundert*, Munich.

Die Künste im Technischen Zeitalter, Gestalt und Gedanke III, Munich.

KURT LEONHARD, *Augenschein und Inbegriff*, Stuttgart.

HELLMUT LEHMANN-HAUPT, *Art under a Dictatorship*, New York.

NELL WALDEN und LOTHAR SCHREYER, *Der Sturm*, Gedenkbuch an Herwarth Walden, Baden-Baden.

WLADIMIR WEIDLÉ, *Les Abeilles d'Aristée*, Paris.

HANS MARIA WINGLER, *Die Brücke*. Woodcuts, Feldafing.

HANS MARIA WINGLER, *Der Blaue Reiter*, Drawings and Prints, Feldafing.

1955 ERHARD GOEPEL, *Deutsche Holzschnitte des 20. Jahrhunderts*, Wiesbaden.

FRITZ SCHMALENBACH, *Neue Studien über Malerei des 19. und 20. Jahrhunderts*, Bern.

HANS SEDLMAYR, *Die Revolution der modernen Kunst*, Hamburg.

HANS MARIA WINGLER, *Der Sturm*, Drawings and Prints, Feldafing.

1956 WALTER HESS, *Dokumente zum Verständnis der modernen Malerei*, Hamburg.

BERNARD KARPEL, *Arts of the Twentieth Century*, A Bibliography, New York. To be published shortly.

LOTHAR SCHREYER, *Erinnerungen an Sturm und Bauhaus*, Munich.

LEXICONS

Allgemeines Lexikon der Bildenden Künstler, edited by ULRICH THIEME and FELIX BECKER, Leipzig 1907-1950.

EDOUARD JOSEPH, *Dictionnaire des Artistes Contemporains*, Paris 1930.

E. BÉNÉZIT, *Dictionnaire critique et documentaire des Peintres, Sculpteurs, Dessinateurs et Graveurs*, Nouvelle Édition, Paris 1948 et seq.

HANS VOLLMER, *Allgemeines Lexikon der Bildenden Künstler des 20. Jahrhunderts* (up till now two volumes), Leipzig 1953 et seq.

Dictionnaire de la peinture moderne, Paris 1954.

Knaurs Lexikon Moderner Kunst, Munich 1955.

PERIODICALS

Pan, published by Otto Julius Bierbaum and Julius Meier-Graefe, 1895-1900.

Simplicissimus, published by Albert Langen, Munich 1896-1944.

Deutsche Kunst und Dekoration, published by Alexander Koch, Darmstadt 1896-1932.

Jugend, published by Alfred Bruckmann, Munich 1899.

Kunst und Künstler, published by Karl Scheffler, Berlin 1903-1933.

Der Cicerone, published by Georg Biermann, Leipzig 1909-1929.

Pan, published by Paul Cassirer and Wilhelm Herzog, Berlin 1910-1915.

Der Sturm, published by Herwarth Walden, Berlin 1910-1932.

Aktion, published by Franz Pfemfert, Berlin 1911-1933.

Der Blaue Reiter, published by Kandinsky and Franz Marc, Munich 1912.

Die weißen Blätter, published by E. E. Schwabach and R. Schickele, Leipzig 1913-1925.

Das Werk, Schweizer Monatsschrift für Architektur und Kunst, Zurich, since 1914.

Zeit-Echo, published by Hans Goltz and Leopold Zahn, Munich 1914-1916.

Kriegszeit. Künstlerflugblätter, published by Paul Cassirer and A. Gold, Berlin 1914-1915.

Das Kunstblatt, published by Paul Westheim, Berlin 1917-1931.

Ararat published by Hans Goltz and Leopold Zahn, Munich 1918-1920.

Der Anbruch, published by O. Schneider and I. B. Neumann, Munich, Berlin 1918-1921.

Ganymed, published by Julius Meier-Graefe and Wilhelm Hausenstein, Munich 1919-1925.

Genius, published by Carl Georg Heise, Hans Mardersteig, Kurt Pinthus, Munich 1919-1921.

Valori Plastici, published by Mario Broglio, Rome 1918-1921.

Jahrbuch der jungen Kusnt, published by Georg Biermann, Leipzig 1920-1924.

Die Schaffenden, published by Paul Westheim, Berlin 1920-1923.

Der Querschnitt, founded by Alfred Flechtheim, published by Hans von Wedderkop, Berlin 1920-1936.

Dada Almanach, for the Central Office of the German Dada Movement, published by Richard Huelsenbeck, Berlin 1920.

Die junge Kunst (monograph series), published by Georg Biermann, Leipzig 1922 et seq.

I. B. Neumanns Bilderhefte, Berlin 1922 et seq.

Merz, published by Kurt Schwitters, Hanover 1923-1932.

Der Kreis, Zeitschrift für künstlerische Kultur, Hamburg 1924-1922.

Europa Almanach, published by Carl Einstein and Paul Westheim, Postdam 1925.

Konstrevy, Stockholm since 1925.

Cahiers d'Arts, published by Christian Zervos, Paris since 1926.

Bauhaus, Zeitschrift für Gestaltung, Dessau 1926-1931.

Le Centaure, Chronique artistique, Brussels 1926 et seq.

Art Lover, published by I. B. Neumann, New York 1928 et seq.

Formes, published by Waldemar George, Paris 1929-1933.

Documents. Magazin illustré, Paris 1929.

Art concret, Paris 1930.

Museum der Gegenwart, published by Ludwig Justi, Berlin 1930-1933.

Omnibus, published by M. Schwichtenberg, Curt Valentin and Leopold Zahn, Berlin 1930-1932.

Abstraction, Création, Art Non Figuratif, Paris 1932-1936.

Bulletin of the Museum of Modern Art, New York, since 1932.

Die Kunst im Dritten Reich (from 1940 *Die Kunst im Deutschen Reich*), edited by the Minister for the supervision of the entire spiritual and philosophical indoctrination and education of the NSDAP, Munich 1937-1944.

Das Kunstwerk, published by Woldemar Klein, Baden-Baden, since 1946.

Bildende Kunst, published by Karl Hofer and Oskar Nerlinger, Berlin 1947-1949.

Réalités Nouvelles, Paris since 1947.

Prisma, published by K. Desch, Munich 1947-1948.

Glanz, published by Bruno E. Werner, Munich 1949.

Thema, published by H. E. Friedrich, Munich and Hamburg 1949-1950.

Art d'Aujourd'hui, published by André Bloc, Boulogne, since 1949.

Jahrbuch zur Pflege der Künste, published by Hans Krey, Dresden, since 1951.

Bildende Kunst, published by Herbert Sandberg, Dresden, since 1951.

Quadrum, Internationale Zeitschrift für moderne Kunst, Brussels, since 1956.

IMPORTANT EXHIBITIONS

1906 First and Second Exhibition of the Artists' Community *Bruecke* in the Seifert lamp factory, Dresden.

1909 First Exhibition of the New Artists' Association Munich, season 1909-1910, Munich, Moderne Galerie Heinrich Thannhauser.

1910 Exhibition of the Artists' Community *Bruecke* at Galerie Arnold, Dresden.
Second Exhibition of the New Artists' Association Munich, season 1910-1911, Munich.

1911 First Exhibition of the *Blaue Reiter*, Munich.

1912 Second Exhibition of the *Blaue Reiter*, Black and White, at Galerie Hans Goltz, Munich.
The *Blaue Reiter*, Franz Flaum, Oskar Kokoschka.
First Exhibition of the Art Gallery *Der Sturm*, Berlin.
International Art Exhibition of the League of West German Art Lovers and Artists, Cologne.

1913 First German Autumn Salon, *Der Sturm*, Berlin.

1920 Dada Exhibition, Dada Early Spring: Paintings, Sculptures, Drawings, Fluidosceptric, Vulgar Dilettanteism, Cologne.

1925 New Objectivity, arranged by G. F. Hartlaub, Mannheim.

1927 Contemporary European Art, Centennial Exhibition of the Hamburg Art Association, Kunsthalle Hamburg.

1937 Decadent Art, Travelling Exhibition, at first in Munich.

1944 *Der Sturm*, Collection Nell Walden, Art Museum Bern.

1948 Paula Modersohn-Becker and the Artists of the *Bruecke*, arranged by Arnold Ruedlinger, Kunsthalle Bern.

Lehmbruck, Macke, Marc, arranged by Arnold Ruedlinger, Kunsthalle Bern.

1949 The *Blaue Reiter*, arranged by Ludwig Grote, Munich.
Art in Germany 1930-1949, arranged by Alfred Hentzen, Zurich.
Contemporary Art in Germany, arranged by Stefan P. Musing and others, Munich.
20th Century Art, The Arensberg Collection, arranged by Katherine Kuh and Daniel Cotton Rich, Chicago.

1950 The Painters at the *Bauhaus*, arranged by Ludwig Grote, Munich.

1951 The Old Masters of Modern Art in Germany, Galerie Ferdinand Moeller, Cologne.

1953 German Art. Masterpieces of the 20th Century, arranged by Ludwig Grote, Lucerne.

1954 Kandinsky, Muenter, Marc, Unknown Works. Arranged by Johannes Eichner, Klaus Lankheit and Hans Konrad Roethel, Moderne Galerie Otto Stangl, Munich.
The *Baue Reiter*, Curt Valentin, New York.

1955 Documents, arranged by Werner Haftmann, Cassel.

1956 From the *Bruecke* to the *Bauhaus*, arranged by E. W. Kornfeld, Gutekunst and Klipstein, Bern.
German Water Colours, Drawings and Prints 1905-1955, Travelling Exhibition through the U.S.A., arranged by Leonie Reygers.
A Hundred Years of German Painting 1850-1950, arranged by Alfred Hentzen, The Tate Gallery, London.

Attention is also drawn to the principal *Annual Exhibitions*: Berlin, Academy of Arts, Berlin Secession since 1893, Free Secession since 1914; Munich, International Exhibitions in the Glaspalast 1869-1934, in the Haus der Kunst since 1949, Munich Secession since 1893, New Munich Secession since 1914; São Paolo, Biennale since 1951; Venice, Biennale; as well as to the various exhibitions of the League of German Artists, and to the annual Travelling Exhibition " Coloured Prints " since 1953.

LIST OF ILLUSTRATIONS

BAUMEISTER, WILLI
Eidos V 69

BEKMANN, MAX
Cabana 64
Self-Portrait 65
Departure................... 66

CORINTH, LOVIS
Walchensee 61
Ecce Homo 63

DIX, OTTO
Portrait of the Poet Theodor
Daeubler 51

ERNST, MAX
Euklid 54
Bird Monument 55

FEININGER, LYONEL
Market Church, Halle 48
Cyclists 50

GILLES, WERNER
Stormy Night 67

HECKEL, ERICH
Reclining Nude.............. 6
Glassy Day 13

HOFER, KARL
Lunares 45

VON JAWLENSKY, ALEXEJ
Heavy Winter 36
The Red Scarf 40
Mountains (around Murnau) .. 41

KANDINSKY, WASSILY
Rider-Improvisation 12 30
Improvisation 34
Street in Murnau............. 42
Composition 43
Composition Red 45

KANOLDT, ALEXANDER
Still-Life 56

KIRCHNER, ERNST LUDWIG
Dancing School 9
Self-Portrait 11
Alpine Hut 22

KLEE, PAUL
House by the Sea 3
Senecio 35
The Window 42
Composition 44
Mask 46

KOKOSCHKA, OSKAR
Venice 58
Portrait of Mrs. Nancy Cunard 59

MACKE, AUGUST
Walk on the Bridge 28
Sailboats 29
Café Turkish II 37

MARC, FRANZ
The Great Blue Horses 24
Two Horses 25
Tirol 26
Fighting Forms 31

MEISTERMANN, GEORG
Tearing Up 72

MODERSOHN-BECKER, PAULA
Self-Portrait with Camelia Branch 5

MUELLER, OTTO
Gypsies..................... 14

MUENTER, GABRIELE
At Sunset 32
Kandinsky at the Tea Table... 33
Man in an Easy Chair (Paul Klee) 39

NAY, ERNST WILHELM
Cromatic, Strong and Tender .. 70

NOLDE, EMIL
Adoration 19
Flowers and Clouds 20

PECHSTEIN, MAX
Still Life 17

PURRMANN, HANS
Flowers 57

ROHLFS, CRISTIAN
St. Patroclus in Soest 21

SCHLEMMER, OSKAR
Group at Banister I 52

SCHMIDT-ROTTLUFF, KARL
Self-Portrait................. 8
Mediterranean Harbor 23

WEIERS, ERNST
Early Snow................. 68

WINTER, FRITZ
Great Finale 70

CONTENTS

On Modern German Painting .... page   5

Documents: Aphorisms, Essays, Speeches ....   »   77

Biographies and Literature on the Artists in this Book ....   »   85

Bibliography ....   »   99

Important Exhibitions ....   »   103

List of Illustrations ....   »   104